M000306336

THE ROAD TO

HAPPINESS

WOMEN'S WISDOM ON LOVE, LIFE & MARGARITAS

Copyright © 2018 CelebrityPress® LLC

All rights reserved. No part of this book may be used or reproduced in any manner whatsoever without prior written consent of the author, except as provided by the United States of America copyright law.

Published by CelebrityPress®, Orlando, FL.

CelebrityPress® is a registered trademark.

Printed in the United States of America.

ISBN: 978-1-7322843-3-3
LCCN: 2018947669

This publication is designed to provide accurate and authoritative information with regard to the subject matter covered. It is sold with the understanding that the publisher is not engaged in rendering legal, accounting, or other professional advice. If legal advice or other expert assistance is required, the services of a competent professional should be sought. The opinions expressed by the authors in this book are not endorsed by CelebrityPress® and are the sole responsibility of the author rendering the opinion.

Most CelebrityPress® titles are available at special quantity discounts for bulk purchases for sales promotions, premiums, fundraising, and educational use. Special versions or book excerpts can also be created to fit specific needs.

For more information, please write:
CelebrityPress®
520 N. Orlando Ave, #2
Winter Park, FL 32789
or call 1.877.261.4930

Visit us online at: www.CelebrityPressPublishing.com

THE ROAD TO

HAPPINESS

WOMEN'S WISDOM ON LOVE, LIFE & MARGARITAS

CelebrityPress®
Winter Park, Florida

CONTENTS

INTRODUCTION

BY BILLUR SUU

"There is no greater agony than bearing an untold story inside you." Maya Angelou, American poetess, memoirist, and civil rights activist

"Every woman has to give birth to herself." Billur Suu, Voyager of Love

"A novelist is someone who is so moved by her experiences that she cannot bear them to disappear into oblivion." Murasaki Shikibu, 11th century Japanese poetess and novelist

"What would happen if one woman told the truth about her life? The world would split open." Muriel Rukeyser, American poetess

I see my daughter's glittering eyes. I feel my husband's awe mixed with joy. Everyone is looking at me as they announce my name, "Billur Suu, Best-Selling Author® of *The Road to Success*." I am in Hollywood, under the spotlights, with an award in my hands. I walk off the stage to my new life. I am a new-born poetess and a writer. When the interviewer asks me, "What does the future hold for you?" I do not hesitate one second, "I am going to be a writer. From now on, all I want is to share my heart."

The book you are holding in your hands has its roots in that sentence. It is my heart's desire to help other women tell their stories: to break the painful silence, to claim the good, the bad, the light and the shadows of our lives, and to pave new paths of happiness, freedom, and female solidarity together. *The Road to Happiness* is a long and winding journey, but it had to be in order to attain wisdom, particularly, women's wisdom.

Why happiness? Happiness as a birthright is a deep belief I've held since my childhood. After many decades of meditation, I also feel that it is our natural state. When we face trauma, heartbreak, crisis, or when we experience loss, it is engrained in our psyches deeper than those happy moments because they are deviations from our normal, happy state. As a happiness seeker around the world for the last three decades, I know that happiness is ours to make, ours to take, ours to enjoy, and most importantly, it is ours to share.

However, when I insist on happiness, I do not mean the pleasure we derive from earthly titles, possessions, or relationships, because their transitory natures create only an illusion of happiness. We may lose our jobs and the power that came with it; our house may burn down; we may separate, get divorced, or simply lose a loved one. True happiness is found within; when we are awakened to the divine presence in our hearts and souls and live our lives as a wonder-filled, purpose-full adventure.

There is one other crucial distinction that lies at the heart of this book, which concerns the difference between intellectual, knowledge and wisdom. One may possess all kinds of knowledge, but not necessarily embrace wisdom. Many spiritual seekers tend to think that intellectual knowledge has its roots in our brain and that wisdom comes from the heart. Indeed, wisdom involves both our intellect and heart. It is the perfect knowledge of life both within and without. We may acquire all aspects of knowledge from outside, yet we have to turn inward for wisdom. Life provides numerous opportunities to gather knowledge from the external world, but it is essential to attain inner knowledge, or wisdom, to satisfy the soul's longing for self-realization. The mystic musician Inayat Khan points out the interesting relationship between wisdom, power, and peace, *"The knowledge of the past gives wisdom; the knowledge of the present gives power; and the knowledge of the future gives peace."*

Why women's wisdom? Women and men perceive and experience life, love, and relationships differently. As a gender-expert with a PhD on the subject, and two decades of work around the world with the United Nations, I previously resented that fact. Now I am thrilled about it, because if we were the same, life would be dull, uninteresting, and not challenging enough for us to evolve as human beings. I was fortunate to meet my soul mate and share a life together for more than two decades. My passionate love story with him evolved into compassion with two life-changing betrayals, which brought me into the presence of divine love. After many years of observation, I believe that women and men are at different stages of evolution and I've learned to seek harmony with the other sex by not taking their imperfections personally.

And margaritas? I've always felt that life gave me lemons, but instead of making lemonade, I went one step further and mixed myself a delightful margarita. If you've ever tried a margarita, straight up, no ice, with salt, it is a mixture of different senses and tastes. You see, where I was born, I had only one choice in life: to be married. Looking back over my half century on earth, I have always combined my heart's desires with my mind's abilities and have ended up living a spiritual life, a soul-full adventure. Although being a writer is my new passion and mission, because it heals others and myself, I feel it is far from being the last stop on my Voyage to Love. I am ready to experience and express my talents and gifts in different parts of the world, involving different senses, sounds, and sights.

Each life is a timeless adventure, offering wisdom, folly, sorrow, and laughter. In this book, we invite you into our lives, story by story. It is our desire that you find inspiration, light, meaning, hope, and resolve to live your life as a wise woman. When I set out to invite other women to share a magical journey into writing with me, I had one goal in mind: when we share our stories, we shall inspire other women to accept theirs and be empowered in ways they never thought possible.

In my humble opinion, a wise woman is an explorer who:

✓ Takes 100% responsibility of her physical, emotional, mental, and spiritual wellbeing and life choices
✓ Asks deep questions about life and her mission in life
✓ Knows what she wants in life and acts courageously, guided by her heart
✓ Determines her own worth based on love connections she makes and beauty she creates for humanity as a whole
✓ Paints her future today based freely on her past lessons and experiences
✓ Taps into her own inner wisdom when faced with adversity
✓ Releases any emotional toxic residue and moves forward in life resentment-free by choosing and practicing forgiveness
✓ Finds perfect love in her imperfect relationships and does not take the weaker sex's imperfections seriously
✓ Always and always shares her wisdom with younger women.

In this book, you shall meet exceptional women sharing their voyage to love with you. In the first chapter, I ask a basic yet fundamental question: how far would you go to search for happiness? I chose to follow the wisdom I felt in Helen Keller's words, *"Life is a daring adventure or nothing,"* and decided to travel solo for fifty days around the world for my fiftieth birthday for an enchanting spiritual pilgrimage.

Chapter two takes you on an artistic journey where you meet a young ballerina, Celine De la Roche, who finds the light in a life-changing accident. We may feel the victims of life's circumstances or rise to the occasion and discover a new path, an authentic calling, or a delightful passion, as Celine did.

In chapter three, Aline Dalbiez takes you to the French Riviera and shares how she had to choose between her health and the man of her dreams. You will discover how to make such a crucial choice, unlock your bliss in every aspect of your life, and finally get everything you ever wanted, including the margarita recipe of happiness.

In chapter four, Chantal Läng shares her heart-warming story of how she found joy, meaning, and happiness after she lost her husband, best friend, soul mate, and the father of her two children. Chantal determines, "All moments of happiness are treasures; they are the diamonds in our hearts."

In chapter five, Patricia Heredia recounts how being an empathic person has been the most profound blessing for her. It demanded that she woke up and not only did she listen deeply, but also felt everything in her life so profoundly. The heightened feelings, beliefs, and experiences taught her what she needed to share with others: how to heal ourselves.

In chapter 6, Ihsane Bekkaye takes us on a journey into the dichotomy between what we commonly identify as feminine and masculine values and concludes that privileging the masculine principle resembles trying to applaud with a single hand. She discusses how the earth and our hearts need the harmony between those feminine and masculine values and how we can redress that imbalance that deprives us from happiness, love, and self-love.

In chapter 7, I share my hard-earned lessons on my Voyage to Love with younger women, from taking 100% responsibility, to achieving dreams, from reaching stillness through meditation, to choosing dark chocolate as an ultimate short cut to live life as a wise woman

In chapter 8, we follow Yody Torres to Turkey, a country that awakens her spirit more than any other and fills her with a sense of home and belonging. Yody encourages every woman to feel inspired to travel and to follow their hearts, especially when it does not make sense.

In chapter 9, Christine Rossi-Flamand depicts the story of a young girl who finds herself with a serious head trauma. We follow her crooked path, from years of rehabilitation for her physical body to wholeness and becoming the strong and wise woman she is now.

In chapter 10, Laura de Waal shares her first trip to Laos and her belief that travel allows you to view yourself, and the world around you, with new eyes. Much like a painter sometimes needs to step back to view their painting from a new perspective, travel allows you to step back and view your life from another perspective, according to Laura. Discover Laura's world as she shares what inspires and feeds her soul's happiness.

Chapter 11 recalls how I gave birth to myself, and why travel is the best medicine to heal a broken heart. My travel to Peru, particularly the few days I spent in Machu Picchu, changed the whole course of my life and helped me to go beyond not only heartache but also taught me a big lesson on what heart-full living means.

This book is the result of a collaborative effort and passion shared by women who come from seven countries with a myriad of backgrounds, ethnicities, professions, and spiritual beliefs. We had but one shared trait: the courage to step out of our pasts, and the experiences life brought us, and the desire to create a new story for our lives. I hope you enjoy your Voyage to Love with us and feel empowered and inspired to create your own path to happiness. Cheers (with or without a margarita)!

CHAPTER 1

HOW FAR WOULD YOU GO TO SEARCH FOR HAPPINESS?

BY BILLUR SUU

"I can't do it. I simply can't take another step!"

My Bhutanese guide was perplexed, startled, and possibly annoyed by my declaration. The sun was setting over the Himalayas, and Bhutan's famous landmark, the Tiger's Nest monastery, was disappearing behind thick clouds. My knees were giving out, the pain in my lower back was excruciating, and the cramps in my stomach were worsening. What was supposed to be one of the best days of my life had turned into a nightmare. Then, something inside me gave up the struggle, and without another word, I walked another four hours to come down from the mysterious monastery. I dropped the struggle, but wished I could drop the turmoil, pain, and cruel betrayal I felt in my bones in the same way. If only I could forget why I had to come on this journey in the first place (as a last resort to save my dignity and my daughter's sanity). If only I could cut the bond I felt to my beloved, who had turned into a madman, a skirt chaser, and a selfish, rebellious teenager after two decades of life together. If only I could drop him out of my life, out of my heart, out of my cells. If only I could drop him.

That day in Bhutan was the beginning of my fifty days traveling around the world solo. I was seeking happiness, which I thought I had lost. This was the birth of a heart poetess and the writer that I feel I am today. This was the beginning of a voyage to love, in the light of my soul and in the company of my heart. This was the beginning of my commitment to share my story so that other women can accept their stories more easily and find the light sooner than I did.

My voyage to love started in the cobblestoned streets of Istanbul. As a young girl, I used to play soccer with my brother and his friends, and use an Ottoman Empire castle as a playground. Then, one day in a local mosque, I was told that I was a girl, thus I had to sit at the back of the room. I was only six years old and I vowed to grow up and show everyone what a girl could achieve. Almost three decades later, despite great odds, I had achieved all my dreams: a PhD from an Ivy League university on women's empowerment, a United Nations career advancing gender equality worldwide, a soul mate who respected my freedom and shared my values, a lucrative income, an ability to travel to more than one hundred countries, and finally the deepest desire of my heart: being a mother.

After working for a decade in Central Asia to bring safe water and dignified sanitation facilities and to empower women and youth in marginalized villages, a trip to Australia changed the course of my life. During our long drive from Sydney to Daintree forest in tropical Queensland, I kept meeting women who asked my advice on happiness, meditation, peace, and relationships. Such encounters intensified as we settled for a month in a little town called Trinity Beach. A young woman I met on the beach expressed her desire to learn from me, but she also stated that she had no means to travel to France, where I was based at that moment.

The next day, during a sunrise meditation, it occurred to me that I had earned my freedom to follow my heart. If she could not come to me, I would go to her. I told her that I would come back to Australia if she could organize a small group of women interested in learning my happiness secrets and techniques and that the course would be a gift to her. When she enthusiastically responded to my idea, I gave myself two months to prepare a foundation course that included daily practices, practical tools, insights, and wisdom to empower physical, emotional, mental, and spiritual aspects of our lives. But before that, I asked my, then 12-year-old, daughter if she would be okay with that decision; I'd have to be away from home at least six weeks and I would miss her birthday for the first time. Her eyes glittered at the idea and I realized that once you give a strong foundation to your child for the first seven years, then another seven years she can grow her wings and grant you the freedom to follow your own dreams.

My two-year full-time study with different spiritual teachers in India, Thailand, and particularly in Canada—with aboriginal leaders—had taught me essential life skills and techniques of self-awareness. These came in extremely handy as I designed my course on heart-full living. I called it "School of Happiness" because I deeply feel that we are here on Earth to be happy. It was also called "School" because we had to unlearn in order to learn new ways of being and acting in this world (my previous two decades long education had fallen short when it came to facing life crises such as infertility, breast cancer, infidelity). My first Cannes School of Happiness courses took place in the heavenly surroundings of Trinity Beach in Australia, and gifted me with a spiritual grandmother who was the first student registered for the "I Love Myself" course.

In 2015, I felt I was at the top of the world: a proud mother of a talented ballerina, a happiness teacher who shared heart-full techniques in the four corners of the world, and a deep sense of satisfaction to know that I was fulfilling my purpose and touching the hearts of my students. My perfect happy world turned upside down in a matter of two weeks. My daughter fell during a ballet class and received a serious injury in her knee. I stopped everything for six months in order to help her heal. To make matters worse, my soul mate went through a temporary period of madness while working abroad; he started running after girls decades younger than he was and I could not leave my daughter alone to go and help him. I did not understand what I had done to deserve such hardship. Why had God bestowed upon me such a terrible ordeal?

I woke up in tears or in poems for months. When I saw nothing was changing, I remembered Gandhi's wise words, "Be the change you seek in the world." I knew I had to give birth to myself again. I knew I had to love myself again. I knew I had to go deeper and beyond to understand the drama and darkness that enveloped me for days and nights.

For me, there was one way out of this senseless tragedy: travel. I sold my diamonds and bought myself an around the world ticket. I'd celebrate my fiftieth birthday by traveling solo for fifty days. I chose five destinations that I had never been before: Bhutan, Ayers Rock, Bora Bora, Machu Picchu, and Santa Fe. In each destination, the right answers emerged by themselves when I dared to ask the right questions.

Bhutan: A new kind of divinity or a new kind of love? On a sunny September afternoon, I landed in the heart of the Himalayas, a majestic and mystical happiness country. I discovered a country a thousand miles apart from the overly romanticized tourist photos. I met with monks, young or old, glued to their smart phones. I struck up conversations with divorced single mothers and witnessed the dilemma of youth squeezed between material reality and spiritual upbringing. But most importantly, I learned that divinity is about accepting our materiality, our humanness without resistance, or labeling, or judgement. No separation. If you apply this rule to love and relationships, there is no you and I, no lover and loved, we are all one.

Ayers Rock: Wholeness or timelessness? It is a living temple that emerged over 900 million years, not a rock! I was fascinated staring at the ruby land of the Anangu people; the colors and people were enticing. I learned how to do a dot painting from an aboriginal elder woman and painted my future. As the sun set with thousands of colors, I took my seat at the Sounds of Silence restaurant. We are instructed to stay silent. Energy changes around silence...like death...like life...deep silence envelops all of us. I lifted my head to stare at the Milky Way from the southern hemisphere. I felt myself between earth and heaven and I let go. When I returned to my senses, I felt that for the first time in my life, I am not missing anything or anybody. I had carried my loved ones in my heart, in my thoughts, in my conversations with myself for the last two weeks. Silence had seduced me, they all had disappeared. After years of meditation, a moment of eternity touches me. I slept well that night, discovering that detachment is the best gift we can give to our loved ones and ourselves.

Tahiti: Am I still beautiful? It was some of the coldest days in the history of Bora Bora. It was raining, windy, and I hardly slept in my beach bungalow. Nature was roaring. In a little beach shack, I saw colorful, homemade rum bottles. I drank some to get warm, and let the ocean wash away my sorrows. I felt even a deeper shift here. I did deep breathing exercises on the beach to take the beauty inside: The majesty of nature, the colors just swallow you...breathe in...breathe out. Some days I stayed in silence, listening to the wind, waves, and birds. My inner voice was softer. Without realizing it, I was re-born, reconnected to the depths of my soul. I felt beautiful, inside and out.

Peru: Which path to take? Following the Inca trail at 10,000 feet high, my soul had one single concern: Which trail to follow and which trail to leave behind? How to let go of the past? How to find harmony again, within me and with my circle of love? In Cusco, I found a spiritual center and joined them for a sunset meditation. Our guide said, "This meditation is causal, ask all your questions and you will get your answers." The next day, I skipped lunch and climbed the mysterious Machu Picchu twice. I gazed into the Lost City and stayed until the guards gently accompanied me to the exit. I received three magical signs, or responses, to my one essential question. I was perplexed, but not surprised. My heart was open to welcome the guidance of the Universe. My path was clear as Billur waters.

Santa Fe: What does it take to be yourself? *How Georgia Became O'Keeffe* is a book that fascinates me. How do we find ourselves or create ourselves? A trail blazer, a loner in the desert, a painter, a woman like no other. Along with Frida Kahlo, O'Keeffe is one of my idols. They were women who dared to live authentic lives. Exposed to overly sensual interpretations of her paintings, Georgia took shelter in Santa Fe's red rock energy. I drove from her museum to her home to her studio to her ranch. Freedom was in the air: the freedom to be yourself. This is the gift I received on the footsteps of O'Keeffe. I dared here; a different kind of courage shone in me. I knew that my silence had come to an end. I need to speak up, share, and help to heal broken hearts. While our relationships may be dysfunctional, love never is.

When I returned from my trip, I knew I had to share my enticing journey to inspire others, especially women who had suffered heartbreak and had lost hope in love and life. About one month after my return, I opened my computer and eleven book titles, including one-page summaries, flew across the keys effortlessly. There it was another sign clear and loud from the Universe: write!

Now I dedicate myself fully to giving life to books on love, life, relationships, and parenting. I believe my writings will be the nectar for those perplexed souls suffering in darkness, as I was once asking God one persistent question: WHY?

Now, I know why. I am grateful for being the one who was chosen for this daunting, but intriguing, task: demystifying half of humanity for the benefit of the other half.

About Billur

Billur does not walk on water (yet), but paints on water. When she was six years old, she realized that she was born to be happy, but felt squeezed by her religion, gender, culture, class and social obligations in Turkish society. At the first opportunity, she spread her wings and flew away in search of the meaning of life and the purpose of her existence. United Nations expert, Ivy League professor, women's rights specialist, poetess, writer, lover, mother, wife, soul mate, yogini, soul doctor, spiritual awakener, and voyager of light are just a few of the roles she's played for the last five decades. Describing herself more of a student of life than a teacher, Billur founded Cannes School of Happiness to help other women to live authentic lives from their hearts.

Called a "soul doctor" by her students and love circle, Billur is a unique spiritual leader and teacher. She integrates ancient wisdom with modern-day scientific knowledge. Her spiritual retreats empower her audience with practical tools, insights from her own life, and creative heart-full solutions. She is the guide you need when you feel broken by, or lost in, a relationship. If you need to stop a drama that's eating you up alive, or discover who you really are, Billur is the best person to help you.

Passionate about helping other women, and sharing her amazing transformation from the darkness to the light, Billur wrote her story in Jack Canfield's book **The Road to Success**, for which she earned a Quilly® award for becoming a Best-Selling Author® in 2016. This was a turning point for her. She now dedicates herself full time to write books on love, life, relationships, and parenting. Her second book, *The Woman Who Sold Her Diamonds and Became a Voyager of Love in Fifty Days around the World*, and accompanying poetry book *Loving You Until the Last Drop: Fifty Love Poems for Fifty Days around the World*, are published by Voyage to Love Corp., a company she established for graceful living and heart-full sharing.

In the summer of 2018, Billur is initiating a new dream project in Central Asia and Africa: building hand washing stands for 1,000,000 school children who live in marginalized villages. This project is the result of Billur's previous work of empowering women and youth through a community water project that she initiated and managed for a decade in 45 villages. Hand washing with soap is a simple act that prevents more than half of children's infectious diseases. She is pledging 50% of all book sale proceeds to this new dream and is inviting you to become a Voyage to Love Water Ambassador.

Billur holds a PhD from Columbia University in the city of New York on social policy and women's empowerment and has won several prestigious awards for her academic and development work in Central Asia. She has been selected as one of the recipients of the Woman of Great Esteem award in 2018 in New York. You can follow Billur's inspiring journey on social media @ voyagetolove and learn more about her fascinating Voyage to Love at www. billursuu.com.

CHAPTER 2

FROM A BALLERINA'S SHATTERED DREAMS TO THE LOVE OF OPERA: HOW YOU FIND THE LIGHT IN AN ACCIDENT

BY CELINE DE LA ROCHE (REGALLET)

Terrified. That's what I felt once I understood what had happened. I was lying on the ground, in a worn-out ballet studio in unimaginable pain, with my dance teacher was staring at me with troubled eyes. I realized that I had fallen out of nowhere and my left knee was looking monstrous with what seemed as an extra bone sticking out of my leg. Everyone in the class was staring at me, tears were starting to fall slowly down my cheeks but I kept breathing. There was no way that I was going to cry in front of everyone.

Teachers were desperately trying to soothe me by saying that all would be fine and that I should stay calm. But, the truth was, I had to stay still. I had no choice but to stay calm because the more I tensed my muscles, the more I suffered. I was completely immobilized. My mother came immediately, almost fainting when she saw me, and soon I heard the ambulance siren. A few seconds later, the anesthesia made me unconscious and I opened my eyes for a brief moment when the doctors were carrying me toward their ambulance.

I can't remember if I visualized anything, but I can recall that I naively believed that these past twenty minutes were nothing but a dream. I woke up in a small room in the hospital, lying on a bed, my knee was incredibly swollen but back to its normal appearance. And my dearest mother was by my side, anxiously waiting. I stared at my blue ballerina costume with my light pink tights and it hit me. I was only twelve and a half years old, how could such a young dancer be so seriously injured so soon?

Most dancers gravely injure themselves after they are already professionals in a company and are over-using their bodies by working eight to ten hours a day. Yet I still had no idea how serious this injury was or how it would change my life.

I started crying, pouring all my heartache into my tears. Doctors at the hospital told me that I would be back on my feet in a week and that I'd be able to dance again very quickly. I was confused and didn't understand how this could happen to ME. I wasn't even on pointes-the torture instrument for ballerinas-when I fell. I was only executing one of the most basic movements and yet there I was paralyzed by my injury.

I truly fell in love with dancing at the age of eight, while performing in a small kids production of the *Lion King* in Turkey. I had loved performing since I was a child, and being cast as a dancer in this musical was pure happiness. I was incredibly lucky to have supportive parents who listened to me and understood me when I told them the magic words, "Dancing is my passion." I was determined to become a professional dancer and I knew in my heart that this was my path. Since we lived in Istanbul, we knew that if I wanted to become a ballerina, we had to get out of Turkey.

As a start, I applied to Roland Petit's ballet school in Marseille, France but having absolutely no technique, I was rejected in one shot. I came back home feeling devastated. My mother told me one precious pearl of wisdom that I shall always remember, "Dance is in you, we just need to find teachers to help you to get it out."

I took a few weeks break from ballet classes and registered for a ballroom dance course instead. Salsa, cha-cha, and all the melodies of Latin America brought me back to my essence: a love of dance. Summer was approaching and we knew that I had to find a summer ballet school. Luck was on my side and we found a summer program in southern France at the Rosella Hightower "Ecole Supérieure de Danse de Cannes." The name caught our attention because Rosella Hightower was one of the very few Native American ballerinas in the world who reached success and had an inspiring international career. When Rosella was only thirteen years old, growing in rural America, she told her family that she would not only become a world renowned dancer, but also that she would establish a school in the south of France.

The summer program at the Rosella Hightower School cemented my desire to be a world class ballerina. But, I was not yet ready to be accepted by the School full-time. Most girls in the class had five to six years of ballet education, and I had only few months. I had a lot to learn and had to grow as a dancer, both technically and artistically. At the end of the summer program, I and my parents asked the head of the school if she knew any good teachers in Turkey. I needed a full year to prepare so that I could audition for the school. Her response was simple but enigmatic: "A former teacher of mine lives in Turkey now, but I have no idea where and how to get in touch with him. Good luck to you."

At least we knew his name and after a thorough search all over Turkey, we located him in a small resort town in western Turkey.

We got up early one day in August and drove eight hours to knock at his door, asking if he would take me on as his student and teach me everything he knew. Robert had been the director of the Royal Ballet of Flanders in Belgium and had danced with astonishing dancers of his time, including Rudolf Nureyev, Maurice Bejart, Mikhail Baryshnikov, and Natalia Makarova among others. Although he was taken aback, since our request was coming out of the blue, he was kind and intrigued by our family. After listening to our story quietly, he agreed to give me a lesson.

My forty-five minutes with him in his dance studio, with a view of Mediterranean, was breathtaking. He checked my rhythmic abilities, carefully analyzed my toes and ankles, and tested my flexibility. When we came out of the studio, he gave us some good and bad news, "Celine's physical body is not born to be a dancer, her hips are too tight, and she is late starting off in this career. But, when she does something right, there is a light in her eyes that will overcome all these difficulties. Her presence and strong feet are her greatest assets."

The verdict was that he would not teach me because he had found himself a new passion that consumed all his time: horses. But he suggested we meet with his former wife, a Turkish dancer who had been the prima ballerina in the Royal Ballet of Flanders and was now based at the Ankara Ballet and Opera.

For the next eight months, every single Friday we woke up at 6 a.m. and either drove or flew from Istanbul to Ankara in order to get my ballet classes. We would arrive around noon, with just enough time for me to eat a bowl of soup in a restaurant close to the opera house, before getting my lesson for three hours. On Saturdays, I'd dance any time that fit into my instructor's schedule. Then Sundays, I'd wake up at 6 a.m. to get my three-hour lesson before we would rush back to Istanbul and I'd be back at school on Monday.

During holidays we made sure to go to Ankara so that I could take private classes every day and progress more. Even now, I'm amazed at myself and how much determination I had at ten years old. From a chunky child with baby fat, I became tall and thin, resembling a classical dancer more every day. Naturally, after so much hard work, sacrifice, and dedication, I was eager to get into Rosella Hightower's school. Half an hour after the audition, when the news arrived that I had been accepted, I was the only one to cry out in joy.

Yet, two and a half years later, I was lying in bed in my house, crying. I just couldn't believe that such a disaster had happened. For eight days I couldn't move an inch, and my beloved mother had to do everything. When I was slowly able to walk again, thanks to crutches, we went to a specialized doctor who informed us that there was a chance that I wouldn't be able to dance ever again. He also informed us that I needed surgery, but we resisted. We strongly believed that I would heal, slowly but surely, without any operation.

No words can describe the great amount of agony I felt. My dreams were crushed. I had to do kinesiotherapy three times a week, sometimes even more, in order to regain my muscles because, believe it or not, I had forgotten how to walk. Due to the dislocation of my knee, my leg had been completely immobilized for a month. I soon understood that our bodies are the most mysterious instruments, and I noticed how much we take our bodies for granted. More than five weeks later, I had the immense joy of walking again. Every step was pure bliss. I was grateful, but, of course, still uncertain if I would be able to dance as I was once used to.

During my first year in Cannes, I had been singing. I enjoyed it, and singing actually helped me become more musical and more graceful in my dancing. Even though I couldn't dance, I could still sing. Opera had been in my life for a year already and I adored my teacher. Singing gave me hope, and encouraged me to heal, because I knew that only a month after the accident, I had to perform on an island near Cannes in grandiose baroque costumes. I simply loved performing. I think more than dancing I just loved being on stage.

Courageously, I walked up and down the stairs of a lovely, small church in a majestic blue gown that covered my huge knee pad. Singing beautiful baroque arias by Charpentier, I felt truly happy for the first time in a long while. I felt just like Madonna in "Don't Cry for me Argentina," singing from a balcony, reaching out to the people below. The spectators were looking up at me and I was in heaven.

I knew what the purpose of the accident was. It was one of those strange moments when my intuition guided me. I realized, deep in my heart, that this injury was meant to show me another path. My love for singing grew and bloomed day by day, and soon, opera became my PASSION.

After five months of intense kinesiotherapy, I was able to dance again. That pessimistic doctor had no idea what I was capable of. In the first days of my dancing, I appreciated my freedom until the last drop, as my mom would say. I loved it. Dancing was liberating. However, I didn't have the same zest as before. There's a huge difference between LOVE and LIKE. I loved singing with all my mind, heart and soul. I only liked dancing once I was back in the studio. It didn't prevent me from continuing another a year and a half in the same school, but the last year was sheer torture. I knew singing was my destiny.

Yet something else kept me excited and going. At the end of what turned out to be the hardest year of my life, I had a singing exam at my conservatory and the judges decided to move me from the 2nd to the 5th level! Soon after, my teacher told me that the best place for a singing education was in America. My French voice teacher truly believed in me, and she strongly recommended auditioning for pre-college Juilliard in New York. For that whole year I did nothing but prepare myself for the audition. It wasn't easy handling demanding ballet classes, especially when all my heart was in opera.

It was a long year, but soon enough, I was in New York when trees were blossoming in Central Park, feeling peaceful and fascinated by this effervescent city. I wondered where I would've been if I hadn't fallen. I gazed through the windows of Juilliard, noticing the infamous yellow cabs of the Big Apple and the hurried New Yorkers. My heart was beating with excitement. I felt nervous, yet, I was ready.

When I look back, I know that my accident was not an accident at all. It was simply a stepping-stone in my life guiding me toward where I was meant to be, and who I'm meant to be. Music is my sacred path; music is my muse; music is the light I shine onto the world.

About Celine

Celine De la Roche is a voyager of love who has traveled the world since her birth. She is an aspiring opera singer who pledges her talent to bring peace and harmony to the world and make this planet a better place. Born in Canada into a multicultural family, Celine considers herself universal and does not feel attached to any country, region, ethnic or spiritual background. She has lived in Kyrgyzstan, Uzbekistan, Thailand, India, France, Canada, Turkey and has traveled to more than 40 countries since her birth in 2001.

During the first six years of her life, Celine accompanied her parents in Central Asian villages, participating in the opening of drinking water systems and distributing awards to school children in the youth parliaments. In India, she discovered meditation and the art of silence, whereas in Thailand she familiarized herself with Thai dancing and culture.

A few years later, when she was eight years old, she discovered that dancing was her passion and performed as a ballerina in the Turkish children's production of Lion King. With the help of her dedicated parents and ballet teacher, she got accepted into Ecole Supérieure de Danse de Cannes Rosella Hightower to pursue serious dance training. Yet, an unexpected accident led her to a new path and opened the doors to the world of music, but particularly opera. Celine feels her passion for singing is growing day by day.

Celine is very grateful to be currently living in New York City and studying at Pre-College Juilliard in the Voice Department. Celine's first language was actually Russian, since she lived in Central Asian countries, yet she forgot this beautiful language after moving and being removed from a russian speaking environment. She currently sings in French, Italian, Spanish, German, English, Latin and Turkish. Celine wishes to empower young generations to live from their hearts and share with them the joy of music. She wants to invite everyone to discover the depths and all the colors of opera.

In the summer of 2018, Celine decided to bring her love of music to Central Asia, where she organized musical workshops for children living in marginalized villages. More than 100 school children took part in her workshops. Celine deeply believes that sharing her love of music is the best gift she can offer to the world, especially to children living in difficult conditions. She hopes to expand her musical love circle to all four corners of the world and invites everyone to feel the magical healing effects of music. Celine is presently responsible for developing musical programs at the Voyage to Love Foundation.

CHAPTER 3

MAKE A TRUE WISH AND GET YOUR TRUE BLISS

BY ALINE DALBIEZ

IF BELIEVING IS A CHOICE, WHAT IS YOURS?

Somewhere in 2007 or 2008, I faced the most impossible choice ever. I was a young woman who had recently started a good job in a worldwide IT company, obviously with a big career ahead. I had already dared to make an important life decision by renouncing the standard road that awaited me in Paris, instead living on the French Riviera, near the sunny sea. But there were two holes in the picture of my life, and in my heart. I was missing the comfort of good health as well as the happiness of sharing my life with the man of my dreams. **What if I had to choose between the two?** Health or love? Surrounded by the natural beauty of the French Riviera, including the majestic palm trees of Cannes, the hot sensations of the sandy beaches and the lavender smells of Provence, that is the question that kept facing me.

"In the twilight, on the sea, this year in particular, you must make a wish if you see the green ray...because your intention will be multiplied to infinity to help you get what you want..." These words were spoken to me that year. While I did not know if what they said was true, I set aside my doubts and decided to

35

seize the opportunity, after all what if there was a chance it could work?

One evening, I went to watch the sunset from a beautiful spot, I'd be able to see the entire bay of the Riviera. I was hoping from there I'd see this green ray. The lights of the dwellings illuminated the coast and the temperature was sweet. Sitting there I found myself facing the most difficult choice. **If this opportunity was only valid for one wish, which one should I choose?** I had two options:

1. To meet the man of my dreams, whom I had been dreaming of every moment of every day since my childhood
2. To regain my health, which I had lost through the difficulties of life, and from which I had been suffering every single day for several years.

The choice seemed impossible in my head. However, faced with the unique opportunity of wishing on the green ray during this very special year, I could not give up!

I began to imagine my life without one or the other to determine which made more sense:

- I realized that living with the man of my dreams, but without health, did not make sense at all. It was too hard to enjoy life when feeling so bad in my body. Every day of suffering reminded me of how much I did not want to live in this difficult physical condition.
- I realized that living without "him," but with health, actually had a little bit more meaning to me. Even if it seemed useless, I could at least continue to dream of "him" while feeling good in my skin.

These moments of reflection were really intense, as if I was negotiating with the universe itself. With all the courage I could gather at that time, I dared to make my decision.

After inspiration, from deep in my heart, with all the love I could feel for "him" and for my health, I made a firm and precise decision, without the least bit of hesitation. **I agreed to choose health, assuming the fact that it was "my" choice, thus preventing myself to resign into frustration**. I could, instead, let go and have total acceptance of "my" decision. I went so far as to accept the idea of perhaps never meeting "him," in exchange for my health. I formulated my wish and, with all my heart, I spoke it out to the universe. *"I wish to regain my health"*

I took advantage of these magical moments during the sunset over the Mediterranean bay, and then I went back home to sleep.

I could never have anticipated what happened next.

As unexpected as it was wonderful, after a few twists—and a few months—I finally met a man even better in reality than in my dreams. In fact, it is thanks to him that I became able to regain my health. I could've never imagined it happening, but that's what occurred. *[How I met him is a whole other story that, surely, you would love to read. It took place just as perfectly as an inspiring movie scenario. To discover this story, and how to make your own wishes come true, follow me and stay tuned for my next books.]* After daring to let go and accept the possibility of never meeting him, it was he whom I first obtained. By dint of love, gratitude and shared joy in his presence, I progressively got enough courage to find the true way to reprogram my thinking patterns and thus regain my inner balance and health. Here was born our program, *REPRÔG*™.

I did not see the famous "green ray" that night, but I made a true choice, out of an impossible decision. This choice allowed me to be sufficiently determined and detached, which finally lead to getting everything I really wanted. **You too can do it, but don't make your decision lightly. Do your part: make a true choice,** with heart, acceptance and determination. Accept with gratitude that you can only have one wish and make a sincere decision for your single most important wish. You will have taken your first step of detachment.

DON'T EVER GIVE UP YOUR PATIENCE

"The ideal does not exist...one cannot have everything, one must make concessions and resign oneself..." **is the worst consolation I have ever heard. Not only have I discovered that it is false, but in the worst-case scenario, you usually end up believing it and you lose all hope.** I've already experienced this in all areas of my life: in order to live my ideal work, to find my ideal home, ideal relationships, ideal circumstances, and so on. Since we are talking about love, I will continue on using that example, but know that these principles apply to everything you want.

As far as I can remember, I have always dreamed of sharing my life with an ideal man who was like me, so we could understand each other and live together in perfect harmony. Obviously, I have often heard others remind me not to delude myself too much, claiming the ideal was "impossible." I confess; my ideal was so complete and precise in my mind that, in the course of encounters and disappointments, it really seemed impossible.

One day, on my journey, while telling a friend of my disarray, I concluded our discussion by saying: *"You know, if I really happen to meet this man of my dreams, the one who would truly fulfill my heart, then it would mean EVERYTHING is possible, even the impossible."*

It didn't cost me anything to wait!

My faith and determination toward my dream, and against all the objections from skeptics around me, protected that dream and guided me to its achievement. As I write these words, it has been eight years since he and I began sharing our happiness in every moment together. We have the pleasure of being even happier, after all these years, than we were already on the very first date. **Let me show you why and how you can do the same, regardless of the obstacles on your path.**

To make a long story short, the first year he and I shared was idyllic, in total happiness. The second year became complicated. I felt resistance between us, as if we were tugging each other in opposite directions. I underwent introspection with a person who worked with family constellations. When we talked about my difficulties with him, she first told me she could feel we were accomplices, like a couple of explorers who laugh a lot together. She acknowledged my concern and asked me the following:

"Imagining you are both on a raft and that you fall over into the water, if there is adversity, would he catch you up?"

This question echoed so loudly that my whole being was pressed with emotion. I realized that during this stage of our difficulties, the answer was actually "no." I knew he was the one I had been looking for, I knew that living with him was my most cherished wish, but I also realized that he was not ready to be there for me. This cognition was frightfully hard to accept, but it was necessary.

At that moment, I discovered the true meaning of "infinite patience." I realized that his own path and pace could differ from what I had in mind. I made the decision—with all my love for him—to let him make his own way and to accept that maybe he just couldn't get on the road to happiness with me. I considered whether it was better for both of us to surrender, to get back my freedom, and, perhaps, live something else with another.

By searching for the origin of a quote on infinite patience in *A Course in Miracle*, I came across the following paragraph which proves to be the perfect summary:
Now you must learn that only infinite patience produces immediate effects. This is the way in which time is exchanged for eternity. Infinite patience calls upon infinite love, and by

*producing results **now** it renders time unnecessary. [...] time is a learning device to be abolished when it is no longer useful.*

I accepted, without frustration, rather by finding appeasement in total acceptance, that it might not be possible for him to fulfill my dream in this moment of time. Through infinite patience, I got an immediate result. In the following weeks, the past came to an end between us, and flourishment took over. Strengthened by my feeling of detachment, I was able to take my place, assert myself in front of him, and assume my limits. Unexpectedly, it pleased him so much that we laughed a lot about it, and since then we have been the happiest explorers of happiness we know. He is amazingly caring and there for me, more than I could ever have dreamed about.

Whatever we want, it takes time. Sometimes we need to clarify our intentions, sometimes adapt to our own success, or sometimes to detach ourselves from the outcome and just relax in acceptance of the present. Patience is an unavoidable ingredient on the road to happiness. **Happiness is a choice, and if we need time or steps to make this choice, isn't it worthy of patience?**

THE MARGARITA RECIPE OF HAPPINESS

We've talked about wisdom, love, and life, but what is the relationship with the margaritas? Well, this is the recipe!

About a year before I had my driver's license, while I was a passenger in a classmate's car, we had a car accident that took me years to fully recover from. After that, I almost never let anyone other than myself drive, especially during evening parties. I also made the choice to never drink alcohol. I do not particularly like the taste of alcohol, even less the consequences that sometimes arise from its consumption. It is often said that a little alcohol breaks down barriers, so I made the choice to never depend on alcohol to dare to be or act with lightness and freedom of spirit.

Thus I do not really know what the taste of a margarita is like, but I know with certainty the taste of happiness. **Here I share with you the essentials, through the recipe of a margarita applied to happiness:**

1. First, make a decision, as firm and determined as I made to the green ray on the sunset, like a beautiful quarter of lime. Rub with it the edges of your life, like the glass of your cocktail.

2. Soak the edges of your life in a little contrast, like a little fine salt that will contrast your drink. Allow yourself to observe serenely what you do not want and simply draw conclusions.

3. You then need three main ingredients:
   a. A good double dose of love, which will replace the Tequila. It's the main ingredient because it makes the basis of the drink, and therefore the basis of your life. **Love is the essence of life, and the more you love, the more you live.** With love, you will live much better and much longer whatever the circumstances, for luck is an excellent friend of love.

   b. Pleasure along the way takes the place of the triple sec, orange peels macerated in the eau-de-vie. This is what makes us enjoy life, appreciate what we have, and do whatever it takes to experience pleasure in walking the path. Do not wait to achieve and live happiness, you'll be worse off to have found it at the end of the way. **The end of life is nothing but death, and it is better to be ready to give up our ideal to live happiness right away rather than waiting to die.** This book is called *The Road to Happiness*, but in fact I speak about The Road "of" happiness because happiness is happily all along the road itself, not just at the end of the road. It is here and now, all the time. It is up to you to live with joy, and to take as much pleasure as you can in whatever you have at your disposal now.

c. Decisions, clear and determined, are the third essential ingredient, which comes in place of the lime juice. **All along the way you will have decisions to make, and the time you spend hesitating is the time you lose not moving forward or enjoying the path.** So, take your head out of the handlebars and choose your direction at each crossing, then look around you and enjoy the scenery. A true decision is one you feel deep inside yourself, with your heart, your guts, and your emotions. If it is not a definite 'yes', it is a 'no'—and dare to assume fully.

4. You then have to add some ice cubes to your beverage, and shake everything in a shaker, before pouring your mixture into the glass you've prepared with fine salt. The ice cubes keep your head cool, and you have to wait a little bit so that they can transmit their freshness to the drink, in order to drink it at the perfect temperature. The same applies for your life: it is with infinite patience that your results will be immediate. **So it is with patience that you must mix your decisions, your love, and your enjoyment of life, in order to obtain the perfect conditions to savor your ideal life.**

You now know the *Margarita Recipe of Happiness.* Implement it now on what you want the most:
- Which one unique wish will you truly make?
- How will you apply infinite patience to it? With love?
- Where is your joy for your life right now?

Happiness is yours, I wish you a good road!

About Aline

Aline Dalbiez helps people worldwide gain confidence to achieve their ideal life, get rid of burdens from their past, and overcome obstacles to reach what they truly desire. Aline has developed an unusual ability to hear through our words how our brains and thoughts are actually shaping our current reality. Extremely thoughtful, she kindly points us into our perceived limitations so we can blow them away. **People usually tell Aline what they "can't" do and she helps them see how they actually "can".**

Aline began her career within leading worldwide corporations, observing the overall suffering of people and feeling unsure, insecure, and powerless herself. She explored human factors until she found a way to become secure, healthy, and powerful. She then created an independent structure to help her clients reset their natural power of success and redevelop their ability to achieve the impossible.

Aline started ALINEON® (www.alineon.com) in 2010, guided by her conviction that, *"If everyone is well, the world is better™."* She has trained and coached thousands of people and teams to better achieve their goals with much less effort, and much more comfort. Aline has worked with everyone from major corporations to individuals. She has used her scientific and self-development background to build a proven recipe for complete success in relation to others, business, and life itself. People can learn and apply these techniques in record time thanks to her program called *REPRÔG™*.

Aline graduated with a Master of Science in New Technologies, International Business Engineering, and Professional Coaching for Individuals and teams. She is now the President/CEO of ALINEON®, a company specializing in the architecture of change and personal fulfillment. Aline speaks, upon request, as an International Public Speaker and Change Architect. She is an active Leadership Council Member of a worldwide Successful Life Club. She was featured on the national *Radio France Info* as an expert and author of her first book on the power of words. She is also the founder of the renowned, *The Alineon Chronicle*, where she reveals the basic skills that everyone should master to live a truly better life.

From a young age, Aline has been trained in most areas of self-care—like biological decoding of diseases, dream reading, Tapping, NLP, past lives or chakra energy healing—as well as business-care areas—such as Human factors, Lean or Agile methods.

When not busy helping her clients, or deepening her abilities, Aline thrives on being the movie star of her own ideal life on the French Riviera, with her dream partner, enjoying nature walks, traveling, exploring the world, or watching inspiring movies. Aline has always been willing to share the pleasure of life, at least with a man who could truly get along with her and make her laugh and smile all day long. She'd had enough of living in struggle and pain and she found her way to meet him. Now, along with him, she shares with others the secrets to master one's life experience.

To connect with Aline:

- www.alineon.com
- contact@alineon.com
- http://fr.linkedin.com/in/alinedalbiez
- https://www.facebook.com/aline.dalbiez
- https://www.facebook.com/AlineonAndYou

Or, for more information about the Margarita Recipe of Happiness visit: www.alineon.com/margarita-recipe.

CHAPTER 4

MY HAND IN HIS

BY CHANTAL LÄNG

We were all together, glasses in hand and smiles on our lips, but our throats were a little tight as we paid tribute to Frédéric, ten years after his death. Friends and family had all responded to my request of this gathering, and I had asked everyone to tell anecdotes about him. Noémie and Gaétan drank up their words, eager to know their dad better. I felt it was an essential moment for everyone present.

Then came my turn to speak. I said my love for him; I said he would be happy to see us happy. I asked myself, "What if it was to be done again, even knowing that he was going to die?" I would have done things exactly the same. The sixteen years of happiness I lived with Frédéric are a gift of life; a blessing I have received and cherish with gratitude. By continuing to be happy and full of love I honor this gift.

All moments of happiness are treasures;
they are diamonds in our hearts.

****

With my heart beating, I climbed up the stairs in the dark, my hand in his. I saw this boy for the first time in the middle of a group of friends on New Year's Eve. How did our hands find themselves together? I don't know. That's the magic of life.

My sister had said to me, "You will see, he is meant for you," but I could not believe it until this magical moment. I, the 19-year-old intellectual who ran on pure logic, never had a hand create such an effect on me.

Months went by and I'd think back, sometimes, to this precious moment. It lived nestled, warm in my heart.

We met again in spring, on his birthday, with the same group of friends. Then, after exciting discussions and ballads by the lake, this young man—so shy—finally dared to kiss me.

It was the beginning of sixteen years of happiness. Pure love. We were two soul mates, fusional and happy to be. Always in love, always hand in hand—even to sleep.

My soulmate. You are, I am, we are.

****

First year, first pitfall. He spent every evening watching television and I was feeling bored. I suggested other activities, but that did not interest him. I started attending acting, language, and computer classes. Until the day when he protested, "There's no point in living together if we do not see each other anymore."

We were both motivated to find a solution, so we made compromises. I narrowed my classes and I stayed with him more often on the couch, even if I was reading a book instead of watching TV. I loved sitting up against him, feeling his smell and his warmth. On his part, he agreed to go out from time to time to a restaurant, to see friends, and even for a game.

I always loved board games, but he hated them. However to please me, he agreed to try. We finally managed to find one—and only one—that he liked: backgammon. His asset: he played instinct while I played strategy...and he won every time!

Quality moments are the cement of love.

****

Second year, second pitfall. When he drank alcohol, he criticized me in public—while the rest of the time he was adorable. When I explained to him how I was hurt, he felt sorry, sometimes he even cried and always promised me that he would not do it again. Yet, he just kept doing it.

I was losing confidence in him; I did not dare show him my weak points, lest they be turned into ridicule at the next opportunity. Finally I realized that he was doing this to value himself and that I'd better value him in another way if I wanted it to stop. It's me who aspired for a change, so it was up to me to change first. Since then, every time I admired what he was doing, I gave him a compliment. Every time he did something useful, I thanked him. Instead of showing my love with only hugs, I added words.

My aunt Yvette explained to me that everyone has a "pot" of love that can be filled with meaningful lyrics. The pot must be sufficiently full to feel love and goodwill. I filled Frédéric's pot and the atmosphere returned to harmony.

Respect and appreciation are the foundations of a happy couple.

****

Sometimes I could be detestable. I remember one evening when I was blaming him for a stupid logistical problem that seemed to me of the utmost importance. I made it a state affair. The more he tried to calm me, the more I insisted; I dramatized.

He took me in his arms quietly and told me, "I love you." It was incongruous and unexpected. Launched like a locomotive, I continued to proclaim my indignation. Without being dismantled, he hugged me and repeated, "I love you."

Suddenly I burst into tears, melted with tenderness. My logistical problem had resumed its proper place, tiny. And my love had regained its place, enormous.

I'm Sorry, Please Forgive Me, Thank You, I Love You.

****

It was midnight, and we were silenced under a sea of stars. We were lying on a ping-pong table in the courtyard of a beautiful Provencal house. Hand in hand, we watched shooting stars, a true fireworks display. I did not even know what vow to do. I was so happy and serene.

Oh, we loved coming on vacation to this house. The journey was long, Frédéric drove and we talked. We put on songs of Francis Cabrel, I sang while he beat the measure with his foot—on a totally desynchronized rhythm, but who cares after all?

As soon as we arrived, while still opening the doors of the car, we felt the smell of rosemary and lavender and we could hear the crickets sing. What a delicious change of scenery! A wood fire, lamb that rotates on the spit, a glass of red wine; life is beautiful.

Happiness is a sum of pleasures, lots of love and
a dash of serenity.

****

One day I decided to become more feminine. I choose to wear heels, suits and makeup. The behavior of the men around me changed from one day to the next. They held the door for me; they talked to me differently.

The proverb says, "You shouldn't judge by appearance." Yet, "I protest Your Honor; the appearance is mighty effective!" Not only for the entourage: I saw myself differently too, I changed the image that I had of myself.

I wonder what Frédéric thought? I'd like to believe that he was proud of my transformation.

How I feel, how I'm perceived, everything is connected.

****

The first time Frédéric was gone for a few days, I was proudly pretending everything was fine. Deep inside, I felt abandoned. When night fell I cried into our big empty bed; without him I felt incomplete.

Over the years, I became more autonomous, at least, emotionally. The transformation occurred gradually, imperceptibly, with the help, probably, of the various personal development courses I was following.

I was almost surprised when I felt serene, despite his departure. I had won my freedom, without missing a beat of the intensity of the couple! I had my cake and could eat it too. I took the opportunity to hang out with my friends and we both had plenty of exciting things to share upon his return.

Freedom amplifies the flavor of love.

****

The room was packed on this Christmas Eve. Hundreds of guests were seated in front of a good meal, Santa Claus distributed gifts, and a camera crew filmed the event from the stands. When the children began to sing on the stage, our team had tears in their eyes. In our nine months of volunteer work with JCI association, we managed to organize an evening to surround the lonely and disadvantaged people. Frédéric was involved as a disc jockey. We vibrated together in this beautiful event.

The room was packed during the General Assembly of the ski club. Frédéric was directing his first meeting. I knew he was nervous, I could see the vein that was beating in his neck. But he behaved calm and relaxed, everything went well in this friendly atmosphere. I admired him in the spotlight.

We were both very different. We each had our hobbies, sport and DIY for him, volunteering and informatics for me. From the beginning, we agreed that our differences were a force, because they were complementary. Together, we knew how to do everything!

Our differences are riches to share.

****

The years went by, life went on with ups and downs, naturally. There were many trips, happy margarita parties, beautiful professional evolutions, a large villa, and especially two beautiful babies —Noémie and Gaétan—the apples of our eyes, the fruits of our love.

I had chosen haptonomy to prepare for childbirth. We learned together to communicate with the baby that was in my stomach. If Frédéric put his hand in any place on my stomach, the baby would move in order to come and blow the right place, as if to slide his little hand into his dad's big hand, it was magic!

During the birth, he was beside me, holding my hand, always supportive. When you're two, you're strong. And suddenly we became…three. What emotion this tiny baby in his arms created. Bright eyes, he dared not move, upset in front of this little wonder.

Love cannot be seen, cannot be heard, it can be felt.

****

Ruby arrived by magic, a hot July afternoon. Noémie toddled in Pampers with bare skin. She smiled, laid down on the knees of the newcomer, who stroked her back.

We looked at each other, Frédéric and I, stunned in front of this immediate complicity with a stranger.

Ruby spoke the language of the heart, so much more important than her three words of French. And Noémie understood intuitively.

Children have an instinctive decoder;
they feel the goodness of the soul.

****

I always knew that Frédéric had a weak heart, but when he fell sick one winter night, we thought it was the same flu that had struck our colleagues. No. It was a terrible endocarditis, an infection of the heart.

A few days later, just before he went into surgery, I brought our two babies to the hospital. Despite his weakness, he managed to amuse his little princess by sticking out his tongue. He was so proud of his children and he had shown their photos to all the nurses.

I was holding his hand when he fell asleep for the operation, we said to each other, "See you later." His hand in mine again, at the end as at the beginning; the alpha and the omega.

Nine horrible hours later, when the doctor told me he died, I couldn't imagine it. It was a nightmare. I touched him, he was still warm; I kissed him, but I couldn't wake him up. His body was uninhabited, almost an object. I looked at the ceiling...was his spirit still present?

The being is not the body; it is more than the body. It is elsewhere.

****

How could I break the terrible news to our little Princess, who toddled from room to room looking everywhere for her dad? We had to find simple words that a two years old child could understand: "He is dead, that means that he will not return." My baby of five months didn't understand what I told him tearfully, he laughed just happy that I had him.

In the following weeks, my sisters and friends surrounded me with a lot of love, but inside I was devastated. I learned to cheat my emotions. Whenever I felt the enormity of what I had lost, the feeling of emptiness made me so dizzy that I physically could not breathe. Then I'd think of something else, as if I was closing a drawer in my head and opening another. It was my mode of survival, a kind of emotional anesthesia.

At night I would turn around in my bed for hours, wondering how I could imagine a life without him and especially ... if I wanted a life without him?

That's where I chose to live.

****

During the months that followed, I pretended to function normally, but inside I was indifferent to everything. I was waiting. I knew that life would come back to me, that I just had to wait. My aunt Yvette and my friend, Matthieu, had told me so.

When I took care of the children, I could forget everything and be really in the present moment. The mist would rip to let a ray of tenderness pass through. It must be said that Noémie and Gaétan were doing well, thanks to Ruby who helped us as if she was their second mother.

It took a year of patience before I felt like myself again, and then the transformation took place in just a few weeks! My energy came back, I started to feel joy again in listening to beautiful music or in touching cashmere, and I'd get excited for a discussion to make plans.

Life is energy; life thrives, when you let it be.

****

Sadness oppressed my heart, during the sunny January first, my second New Year without Frédéric. I wished he were there, I wanted him to see the progress of the children, congratulate them and hug them.

It was too cold to get out, but too sunny to lament. The sun was pounding through the large bay windows; it was a message of life sent to me by the universe. I shook myself like a dog coming out of the water and jumped onto my feet. I wanted to do something cheerful, and maybe a little crazy.

Seized with a sudden inspiration, I blew up our plastic pool and filled it with hot water...in the middle of our living room! The children could not believe their eyes. They looked at me with open mouths and bright eyes. I was their heroine. I put on some catchy songs, which we knew by heart, and we sang at the top of our lungs, jumping and dancing in the pool—hand in hand all three.

You have the power to create happiness.

About Chantal

Chantal Läng -- Coach, author, passionate student of health and biology, and IT project manager

Chantal is dedicated to helping people recover from chronic diseases, especially migraines and Crohn's disease, by educating them about caring for their bodies in a natural way. When people feel hopeless, after having tried everything, she helps them find priority changes that will benefit them. Passionate about biology, she has been studying the body's functions every night for 20 years. Chantal tests machines and products, follows training courses, and attends natural medicine congresses, where she exchanges with the most experienced professionals. After healing herself of chronic migraines and Crohn's disease, she helped friends and friends of friends before putting her knowledge into video to share with as many people as possible.

During the day, Chantal works at a Swiss Television as an IT Project Manager. She loves this exciting and varied job, which requires—in addition to technical skills—great organizational and communication skills. Convinced that collaboration and mutual aid are the engines of success, she practices kindness on a daily basis and insufflates good moods into her project teams. After her husband's death, Chantal raised her two children alone, teaching them joy, love, and self-respect.

Since 1991, Chantal has been very active with JCI (Junior Chamber International) in Geneva. She has held numerous posts in this volunteer association, which has given her the opportunity to develop a variety of skills and participate in numerous exciting community projects. For her contributions, Chantal received the JCI Senator Award, a worldwide honorary lifetime membership.

Chantal studied multiple languages at Voltaire College in Geneva, Switzerland—including French, English, German, and Italian. She then completed the International Diploma of Project Management IPMA level B, and received a postgraduate degree in Business Analysis. Chantal is also a coach at the University of Geneva HEG for students preparing for their diploma in Business Analysis. She is currently studying web marketing, in order to share her biology skills on the Internet.

You can watch Chantal's videos in French on her YouTube channel "VIREtaMigraine," which means, "get rid of your migraine." They are also available on on www.viretamigraine.com

You can contact Chantal at:

- chantal@viretamigraine.com
- https://twitter.com/Chantal_Lang
- https://www.facebook.com/viretamigraine/

CHAPTER 5

LISTEN CLOSER

BY PATRICIA HEREDIA

I actually prefer a good Manhattan. I didn't always—I had to learn to like it, to appreciate the subtleties, the texture, and the flavor. Mostly, I have learned how important the bitters are, which ones are used, perhaps a combination of different bitters and then, of course, don't overdo it! There are so many to choose from.

Life is like a good Manhattan, you know, it is a finely tuned recipe with so many good variations, ingredients, amounts of this and that, different presentations, different containers, up or on the rocks, one cherry or two, maybe a toasted orange peel. Life without the bitters would, well, just be missing the secret ingredient.

I have learned to value, embrace, and get excited about the "bitters" that come into my life. You want to know what the bitters really are? They are the experiences of everyday life, specifically the ones that hurt us, break our hearts, and challenge us. Of course we have all kinds of experiences: joyful, happy, easy, fun, helpful, comforting. The experiences in our lives are the fuel for growth, the fuel for creating exactly what we desire our lives to be. It is all of life's experiences that propel us forward in this physical reality we call human existence. All experiences are relevant, important and necessary for our growth; our purpose for being here. One is not better than another; there really is not a right or wrong way to grow. That is just a perception, a chosen belief. Everything in our life is a choice, whether you believe it or not, whether you are conscious of it or not, whether you accept it or not. Understanding that you have a choice is FREEING. This is what my life has been about, learning that I am what I am because of the experiences I have gone through, the beliefs that I hold and the choices that I have made –consciously and unconsciously.

So how in the world did I get from point A to, well, maybe point M? I was born in 1950 in a most wonderful part of the world: the State of Michigan in the United States, and right by Lake Michigan. I lived in the middle of a vegetable and flower patch—no kidding. I think about that now—how cool, how abundant, how nutritional! That is not, though, how I perceived or experienced it then.

Of course I was born, like everybody else, blind, deaf, dumb and with amnesia—figuratively, not literally. I am laughing here, but that is how most of us enter a life here on planet earth. What I became aware of is that I was different from others, and there is a name for what I was experiencing. I am an Empath. I had no clues, no concept of what this very natural ability was—only that my life was difficult, lonely, sickly, painful, and contained non-stop anxiety and even rage.

I always felt like an outsider, watching from the sidelines. I was physically sick and emotionally challenged. I absorbed everything around me—other people's emotions and beliefs, illness patterns without understanding what was mine or not mine—from the moment I was born. I was like a sponge, a magnet with no filters.

A clinical description of an empath goes like this: Empaths are emotional sponges that absorb both the stress and joy of the world. Empaths feel everything, often to an extreme, and have few if any guarding filters between themselves and others. As a result, empaths often will be overwhelmed and are prone to exhaustion and sensory overload. Empaths have an extremely reactive neurological system and are super responders. They need alone time, are sensitive to light, sound and smell. Empaths sense other people's emotions, energy and physical symptoms in their own bodies. They are supersensitive to the tone of voice and body movements. They can hear what others do not say in words but communicate nonverbally and through silence. Empaths feel things first and then think, which is the opposite of how most people function in our over intellectualized society. There is no "membrane" that separates them from the world.

Empaths can have spiritual and intuitive experiences and feel premonitions about the future. So you get the picture—all of the above and right from the beginning. You can imagine how well— NOT—any and all of this was seen or received by everybody around me. I learned quickly to become very secretive about what I was feeling and sensing. I learned to suppress what I felt and deny what I knew to fit in, to avoid backlash—it was a survival technique. It became very natural for me to be quiet, watch and listen. I was learning and developing one of my talents, for me the most important one, listening. I needed to learn to listen closer to everything that was going on around me in order for me to know what was mine and what was not, but also to know what people were unintentionally communicating to me. This might not come as a shock to anybody, but people typically do NOT let you know what they are really thinking and feeling. People cannot fake what frequency is vibrating off them—humans offer to the outside one thing and inside feel an entirely different thing, and it is typically done unconsciously. People have evolved and adapted themselves to fit in, be accepted, and even survive in societies. I, however, was feeling and "hearing" more than what most people wanted me to know and I learned to take it in and be very quiet about it. This ability was a difficult key that was going to serve me well in my future work.

All of this, every part of it was a profound blessing. I will repeat that—the challenges were my gifts, my perceived weaknesses grew into great strengths—the challenges of my life, the way to fulfilling my destiny, my reason for being here, were presented to me through the keys of my lessons and challenges: my bitters.

I grew to understand this to be a most beautiful blessing because it was the springboard for my life's work. I was required to live what I was to teach others, but I had to heal myself first. I had to wake up, listen closer, and feel everything slower.

I did wake up, in 1988, and I embarked on my metamorphosis: mentally, emotionally, physically and spiritually. I changed myself at a cellular level, rewired my brain—you name it, I did it—and it was slow going. I changed everything about myself and it was a TOTAL IMMERSION PROGRAM.

I started with my subconscious beliefs by using energy work. I did Rebirthing, Reiki, Healing Touch, meditation, journaling, self-hypnosis, and dream work therapy. I even went to a South American healer and had my heart center opened.

The next piece of my transformation was physically detoxing my body, I used fasting, juicing, herbs, homeopathics and manual detox techniques. By the time I was 44 years old I was a different person. At this point, I asked myself how could I make my life's journey my life's work. I felt compelled, called, to help others do what I had done. I now recognize that was my destiny—my calling—pushing me forward.

So, in 1995, I opened a small health clinic in Grand Rapids, Michigan and I am now in my twenty-third year living and doing my life's work. It is my purpose for being here and it has been a long road over a very long time. A large part of my work has been as a hypnotherapist and coach. I help people change and heal themselves from the inside to the outside. I help them change their minds, their thinking, and their belief system.

That is the most important key I can share with you: heal your belief system, your thoughts, and your mind. Release any and all limiting beliefs, thoughts, feelings, blocks and resistances. These are perceptions only—our own, our parents, our communities, our countries, our cultures, other people's perceptions/opinions— nothing more. Once the resistances are released allow yourself to receive all of the good that is, and always has been, all around you.

None of us are lacking knowledge or motivation. You are just like everybody else; you have a strong set of limiting beliefs— subconscious—that are holding you back. The subconscious is the largest part of our mind and it rules us. These deep subconscious memories and patterns are limiting beliefs that act like blocks that dictate our perceptions of our reality. Our mind creates the reality we experience, and it is sculpted from these limiting beliefs. The most prominent beliefs we hold, whether positive or negative, create our reality. This happens because we attract to us what is transmitting from us. We build momentum, positive or negative, through the collection of our thoughts, emotions, beliefs and experiences. Our minds take everything in this "collection" deep into our cellular memory bank as if it is true. It literally anchors into our cells, our bones, and our heart and it influences our lives as frequencies. These can be described as mental and emotional programs that are playing on autopilot! We transmit these frequencies, consciously and unconsciously, and we attract to us like energies that affirm and support our own beliefs. If that is not confusing enough, we are also further influenced by the human collective consciousness and past generations.

Now back to the important key of changing your belief system, it is usually the HOW to do this that stops most people from doing anything. Rewrite the script in your mind. Change your mind. Rewriting, so to speak, in this way "that it no longer restricts or harms you" is perfect. Attempting to erase or stuff away your limiting beliefs is not the way. Make peace with them. Become neutral with them. Let go of all resistance. Again, the reason is this: everything in our lives, even when it has been difficult or tragic, has made us who we are and has assisted us to grow. It has expanded our access to love.

So, never desire to erase those experiences. What I am talking about is what I call search and recover. Find these limiting beliefs, heal/release them and then replace them with new instructions, a new "software" program, so to speak. Our conscious mind and belief system absolutely must be congruent with our unconscious mind and belief system for us to be successful. If there is any incongruence between our conscious and our unconscious, we are destined to keep repeating the same behavior over and over. So, how does this work and how do you do this?

First, how does this work: When we revisit any of it from a spiritual, higher perspective, accept full creative responsibility, forgive ourselves and all others involved, give gratitude and thankfulness for the experience and send love to ourselves and all involved we change it. We no longer have that negative attachment in our cellular memory. What we experienced and what it taught us, the purpose of the experience, is kept. It is balanced and the negative aspects of it are energetically released.

How do you do this? It is actually simple, but it takes practice— consistent, methodical practice for a long enough period of time to form a new habit. The "poke it with a stick" method will not work. When anybody thinks/feels/does anything regularly, repetitiously, for a long enough period of time the neurology of the brain changes. The brain can and does change, it is called neuroplasticity, and a new habit is formed. The change happens when you heal your subconscious belief system, allow yourself to receive the good all around you, practice your practice and build momentum. By practicing your practice you build momentum, they go hand in hand. Practicing your practice means to focus attention on your thoughts and feelings. Listen closer to your intuition and higher guidance. Steady and deliberate quieting of the mind, moving through your day, following your inner guidance—even 68 seconds of focused mindfulness will carry the momentum. Meditate, play, learn new challenging things, journal, program yourself through Hypnosis and affirmations, heal limiting subconscious beliefs through NLP and other healing energy protocols, dream build by placing yourself in the middle of what you desire, travel, listen to music, read, listen to guided imagery recordings, place yourself around others who have what you desire and are where you want to be.

When you meditate, simply sit, feel and listen to yourself. There could be energies of love, resistance, awkwardness, pain, anger, sadness—just recognize and observe. Attach to none of it. Let it pass right through as if it is on a conveyor belt. Simply sit with what you are feeling, thinking and experiencing until it feels more neutral—it is just a perception. When you know your own energy, and simply sit with it more frequently without any judgment, you open yourself up to receiving messages from your higher consciousness. You will feel clarity, an inner guidance. Also, negative thoughts and emotional patterns will manifest less frequently. You will gain a greater sense of knowing about the true nature of any situation. Clarity is freeing.

Disconnect from outer happenings around the world, negative people, and situations—cut the cord—free yourself. It is essential to be proactive and protective of your energy. Speak up, let go, move on, and change. Any attention to the negative is holding it right in front of you—what has been is done, it is past, let it go, forget about it.

Suspend the need to know where life is headed or how things will play out. Release yourself from the responsibility of making what you desire happen—the how—or anxiously striving for the solution. Be completely at peace with exactly what is flowing around you. Trust yourself above all others and trust your intuition, which is your own higher guidance.

Get Happy! See the humor in everything. Anger weakens your

immune system and laughter strengthens it. Find a starting place where there is some movement toward feeling happiness, peace or joy. Then focus more and more on this happy, peaceful place and the momentum builds. You will begin to transmit a positive frequency and then more momentum builds. This is proactive creating at its best—be deliberate for your vibrational frequency.

There is a shift happening for everyone and everything. There is no just staying put or even going back. I have been speaking of a way to heal yourself and move through this shift. The best that I can hope for is that what I have shared about myself, and my path, can be of benefit to you and perhaps shed a light on your own path.

Thank you and blessings - Patti

About Patti

Patricia Heredia is the founder of The Therapy Center, an alternative health and detoxification clinic in Grand Rapids, Michigan. She is also a contributing writer for Star Nations Radio Network and Magazine.

Patti has been a therapist in the alternative health field for over 25 years. In her practice, Patti offers her clients an opportunity to change their entire lifestyle through multiple services and therapies. In addition, Patti offers an integrated approach to cognitive behavior modification by using Hypnosis, Neurolinguistic Programming and Thought/Field Therapy.

Patti resides in Grand Rapids, Michigan. You can connect with her through her website at:

- www.grandrapidstherapycenter.com

or at:

- Pheredia50@hotmail.com

CHAPTER 6

A SINGLE HAND CANNOT APPLAUD

THE HARMONY BETWEEN THE FEMININE AND THE MASCULINE VALUES, A BLESSING TOWARD A BETTER WORLD FOR WOMEN, MEN, CHILDREN, AND THE EARTH

BY IHSANE BEKKAYE

Did you have a beloved grandmother?

The person that had the most impact in my life was my grandmother. She grew up in the twenties in Morocco; she was Aisha.

Aisha, a woman, illiterate, and visionary, defied the patriarchal system perpetuated by her ancestors. Aisha, illiterate and visionary, thought from the depth of her soul that girls SHOULD go to school. Aisha, illiterate and visionary, was a courageous woman who accepted being humiliated by her family in order for her daughters, and all the other girls, to have a better life.

My childhood was far different than my grandma's. When I was little, my parents did not ask me to prepare the meal, dress the table, make my bed, or clean my room. They did not ask me to participate in any of the housework. Instead, they asked me to work, and to work hard. More precisely, they asked me to have the best grades in the class. Work was my childhood commandment. And it worked quite perfectly, I had A or A+ everywhere.

When I was a teenager, I had a very painful insight. In life, there were only two categories of people: those who crushed and those who were crushed. I did not want to crush; it is not in my nature, at all. For those who are keen on astrology, I have four planets in the sign of Cancer, which gives me a huge sensibility. But I did not want to be crushed either. I did not want to be at the mercy of the adults, especially males, who did not hesitate to harass and abuse girls. Which had happened to me more than once.

My dear grandma had a saying, "Arrajal Kbour," which literally means Man Grave. She believed that marriage is like a grave. You cannot get out of it, until death separates the two. It doesn't matter if you don't get along together anymore, or you become only roommates. Who cares? You stay anyway. The most important thing is that the appearance of the marriage is preserved.

So, in my little teenager head, I made my plan. Even if nature gave me a girl's disposition, I was going to transplant myself and learn to use a boy's mentality. I was going to get tough, to harden myself, and set aside all this weakness—this pretty-pretty insipidity of women. There I was, going through life with my distorted vision of reality. My head full of diktats and my warrior suit…not quite the portrait of a young, well-educated girl.

Sartre said, "Hell is other people." Sister Emmanuelle said, "Paradise is other people." Years, and thousands of hours of personal work, later, I understand that hell is the exclusion. Hell is walking on a single leg when you have both. Hell is cutting a part of oneself. Hell is thinking that one's birth equipment is inferior to another's. Hell is believing all the false statements that we are told.

Have you ever thought that your right hand is better than your left hand? That your left eye is more valuable than the right one? Ladies, is your left breast better than your right? Those are absurd questions, aren't they? Really absurd. Yet surprisingly, for millenaries, that's the way it has been. Culture maintains that the Masculine principle is superior to the Feminine principle and, as a consequence, that men are superior to women. This was the start of tremendous trouble.

You see, on one hand, there are women and men, people with a feminine or masculine sex. On the other hand, there is the principle, the polarity, and the values of the Feminine and the Masculine. Men mainly bear masculine polarity, and woman bear feminine polarity.

What are those values?

Feminine values	Masculine values
Relationships	Action, Results
Feelings	Expression, Wording
Openness	Decision
Soul	Sense, Reality
Kindness	Structure, Law
Intuition, Receptivity	Facts, Analysis
Inside	Outside

Privileging the masculine polarity is terrible for men, children, and the earth. It is even more terrible for women, because they amputate a main part of their identities to better identify with those masculine qualities.

Let's get back to what I said about myself in the beginning, so I can elaborate on what I meant by saying I was focused on being the Masculine. I privileged action, performance, work, results, and career achievement over relationships, openness, vulnerability, and alterity. I chose the outside, what was expected from me, rather than the inside, my inner, deep aspirations. The cost was expensive. Very expensive. For you cannot ignore with impunity what yells inside you.

Privileging the Masculine values over the Feminine is like being the crimson man who told the Petit Prince, "I am a serious man. I am a serious man." However he was a man who never did anything other than additions, who never smelled a flower, who never looked at a star. Privileging the Masculine principle is like trying to applaud with a single hand.

So how do we rehabilitate the Feminine values? First by being aware that we, women and men, are granted the two polarities. They are complementary, different, equally useful, and nice. We can say anything about one or the other, except opposing them in terms of superior and inferior.

I would like to take the example of the conception of a child. The Masculine fecundates, the Feminine welcomes. The Masculine protects, the Feminine surrenders to the process without trying to intervene during the nine months. Without action, without the life power, without protection, which is to say, without the Masculine, there is no newborn baby. Yet, without receptivity, patience, and surrendering, i.e. without the Feminine, there is no newborn baby.

When a woman is pregnant, she is not asked to pull up the baby in order to make him grow faster, or to monitor his growth, or to have weekly meetings to make sure targets are achieved. If we keep only two things to define the Feminine, it is the importance of relationships and receptivity, surrendering to what is.

Why don't we model what God (or Nature, the Universe, Life, etc. according to your beliefs) makes work so perfectly? Why, for us, for human beings, even if we have the directions of use for the

"Belle Oeuvre," does it work so badly? The planet is damaged: the air, the oceans, and the lands are polluted. Money is ruling the world.

In many places of the world, human beings are ill treated, humiliated, and exploited. Women are raped, excluded from their civil and human rights, and considered as inferior and impure. In 39 countries in the world—and this is only one example among hundreds of discrimination–women inherit less than men. For example, in my childhood country of Morocco, a woman inherits half a part and a man a full part. I am ashamed of that.

On another topic, two major acts of life, i.e. birth and death, have gone from quick, natural processes to long, medically assisted ordeals. Humanity has a hard time having babies and dying. Do you wonder what the link between women's exclusion, money, pollution, and the difficulty to die is?

There is only a single link, the exclusion of Feminine values. Feminine principles are being set aside, creating Masculine hegemony. The Masculine and the Feminine, when working and walking hand in hand, ensure balance, harmony, and justice. The Masculine alone becomes insensitive, extreme, tyrannical, and unaware of its behavior's consequences on people. It lacks its alter ego, its "sweetener," and its heart. The Feminine alone, lacking its alter ego, is soft and unstructured. Often playing the victim, becoming passive, dependent, and perpetually complaining.

How do we leave this mortifying unbalance that deprives us from happiness, love and self-love? First of all by acceptance and the willingness to take a systemic glance. The nice women and the bad men are only in the movies. In reality, all of us, men and women, make the patriarchal system that oppresses us prosper. Yes, even, us, woman, are truthful and loyal to the system that undervalues, demonizes, condemns, and breadcrumbs us.
The very first transformation stems from education. And regarding education...I beg the mothers, the numerous mothers

71

that have invested their motherly function as a place of power to compensate the oppression that was put upon them. I implore them to stop deifying and making a god of their sons, thus raising psychically immature men facing all-powerful sacrificial mothers. I implore them to stop raising little abusers and victims looking for a tormentor/ savior. By looking to their sons with enamored eyes, they are making their sons feel superior, untouchable, and granting them impunity for their behaviors, making them think they are above the laws. While their daughters are hardly looked at, yet are asked to contribute a lot.

I also urge, the fathers to take their place—to play their masculine role, of the separative third. This function stops the temptation of every mother to be only that, to be one with her child, especially her son. The father is the separative third in the triangle father-mother-child. He allows the existence of the relationship, of another one in the pair mother-child. He helps the child understand that the mother is not his alone and inversely. He helps the child to differentiate, to build his own identity, to go to the outside world. He encourages him and challenges him when the woman could be more cuddling. He also plays a role of a "forbidder," of a law bearer.

In France, in 2018, a gynecologist shared that during the echography, when he announces to the parents that the baby is a boy, the reaction is different. There is more joy, more pride than if it is a girl. How can we help stop this anchored perception of reality? How can we stop contributing to the depreciation and sometimes, even the hatred of the Feminine? How shall we avoid little girls saying, "Why was I born a girl?" To stop mothers fearing having a girl? How can we contribute to the fact that we, women, are happy and proud to be bearing the feminine polarity, to honor it without having to complete 20 years of therapy? How can we trigger the fact that humanity valorizes otherness, openness, welcoming brought by the Feminine principle rather than seeing a threat in it that has to be silenced, covered, demonized, sewed? Maybe you think that I am exaggerating, or that I am describing past centuries behaviors. That this does not exist in the 21st century in Western countries. Men argue: I take care of the kids, I bring them to school, I shop for groceries, and I help my wife.

This is advancement, indeed. But it is far from enough. Today, in the western world, little girls are still victims of sexual abuse. Women are exhausted, at the mercy of predators, and have precarious and lower paying jobs. They are discriminated against for one reason: they are women.

We cannot be satisfied with the current improvements, or tell ourselves that the situation is extraordinary in the West compared to other regions of the world, even if it is true. We cannot affirm that we have attained a satisfying situation, while there is not a single day without the burst of a sexual scandal in the United States, France, England and elsewhere.

We hear, here and there, the expression of a girl's power, women's power. Sure enough, we women should be part of all the decisions: Decisions for the family, decisions for the executive boards, decisions for the city and for the country. We, women should take our legitimate position, our whole legitimate position, and nothing but our legitimate position. The solution is not to replace one excess with another. We do not want the hegemony of men replaced by the supremacy of women. Most certainly, when we look at the women's condition through the world, there is no chance that that can happen.

"La Belle Œuvre," the Great Works, the happy medium, the golden mean is both Masculine and Feminine, hand in hand, balanced. Not too much of either one. The power of the Masculine is beautiful, but in excess it turns into brutality. The kindness of the Feminine is heartening, but in excess it turns into complacency, cowardliness.

Native Americans teach us the beauty of balance and consideration for Feminine values. When they make decisions, they wonder about their consequences on seven generations, which means they care about others. They greatly respect the Earth. It is also one of the very few cultures where women are not impure, especially when they have their periods. Even more, they are blessed. The openness, the respect of the feminine polarity cultivated by the Native Americans cost them an unbearable price facing the colonists who exalted the Masculine principles as a virtue. For most of them (with some exceptions like the Quakers), what was important was the conquest at all costs, at any price. Often, the greatest thing they lost was the value of a relationship.

The relationship is THE characteristic of the Feminine Polarity, so attractive yet so unreachable. The relationship is central to me. I, who was not very successful in my love stories, told myself that there might be a bug in my data processing. Something like, "You have the hardware, but the connection, the wiring was forgotten. The electrician was off!" As a matter of fact, the setting is really there. My untiring, unwavering quest was, "How does a human being work," but not has become, "How does the Feminine and Masculine work? How can we be in the 'Belle Oeuvre' (in balance), how can we harmoniously marry, inside of us, the Feminine and Masculine so that the outside wedding is beautiful?"

I promise you tears on the journey. They'll be tears of sadness, despair, powerlessness and a lack of understanding. More cheerful, they'll be tears of joy, happiness, and ecstasy. Feminine and Masculine, hand in hand, it is the "Belle Oeuvre," the nice bit of work—the hope, the confidence and the LOVE.

We live in an epic time. We have in our hands the map that leads to a heartening, nourishing relationship paradigm, in which love is the king. We need to roll up our sleeves and invent a new model. To renounce some real and fantastical privileges. To establish the Feminine and Masculine, walking hand in hand. Both in heart intelligence and action intelligence. For the friendly hearth (heart and earth).

This chapter tells about the harvest of my journey. I learned piece by piece, easily and painfully, a lot related to the Feminine polarity, which I was lacking so much. I learned to trust, I learned to surrender, I learned to cherish relationships, and I learned that I am not alone. I am part of a bigger plan. I learned to see the Good in God and God in all the Good.

I learned to applaud with my two hands!

About Ihsane

Ihsane Bekkaye speaks several languages. At the age of one and a half, she chatted in French with her parents and in Arabic with her grandmother. At three, she had thorough conversations with her schoolteacher. Even back then, as a little girl, when she spoke, she was listened to.

Her life story, with its joyful moments and its ordeals, surrounded her untiring, unwavering quest around the question, "How does a human being work?" Lately, that question has evolved into, "How do Feminine and Masculine bond harmoniously?" Ihsane is a person that enables others to step aside and open their consciousness by looking at them in an out of the box, stimulating, kind way.

Her conferences, as well as her Tedx talk, are about how can humanity be in the "Belle Oeuvre," or in balance. She further explains how we can harmoniously marry, inside of us, the Feminine and Masculine so that the outside wedding is beautiful.

What particularly motivates Ihsane is women's transcendence past old-fashioned patterns and helping them access their personal realization, with more love and esteem. It is the core of her message: guiding women towards their greatness and full potential.

A single hand cannot applaud; this is a Moroccan saying that she heard a lot when she was a child. Her deep aspiration is that we all learn to make our two hands applaud together, like two hearts. Those two hands are the Feminine and the Masculine, and their harmony and balance is THE condition for a better world for women, men, children and the earth.

Ihsane has a degree in Human Resources Management from the famous Paris Dauphine University. During her corporate life, she was a HR executive in multinational companies. Then, as a coach and a facilitator, she's worked with executive teams and people in several countries. She has a serious education in personal and spiritual growth and has several certifications in

Coaching, team building, Enneagram, Human Element, Radical Collaboration, etc. Her journey has a strong background with the Jung's psychology.

Ihsane is a coach, an author, and a speaker. She works with individuals and corporations on Feminine-Masculine Balance.

CHAPTER 7

TAHITIAN PEARLS OF WISDOM FOR MY DAUGHTER AND FOR ALL THE DAUGHTERS OF THE WORLD

BY BILLUR SUU

This is a love story
Like no other
Life-giving, uplifting, mesmerizing
The minute I gazed into your eyes
I knew I was in heaven on earth
And what a journey it has been
My cherished, my beloved, my daughter
My sun, my moon, my angel
I am so proud of you
Not only for what you do or accomplish
But WHO YOU ARE
Loving, passionate, compassionate

79

Dedicated, generous, sensitive
And beauty-full
Inside and out
Challenges come and go
Your new age arriving and it will go
But you will ALWAYS stay
As the best gift I have ever received
In this lifetime and beyond
Happy Birthday
Thank you
For the most wondrous 13 years together

It is a challenging endeavor to attempt to share my wisdom in these pages for my daughter, when I consider her my teacher and inspirer. I wrote the poem above a few years ago to celebrate the love and the light she has brought into my being. The poem is only 112-verse long, which can give you a sense how she moves me deeply.

I feel that bringing a peaceful, happy, openhearted, sensitive, and free daughter into the world is by far the most important contribution I have made to humanity. We give foundation to our children for the first seven years, and if we provide an environment in which they are respected and cherished, then they grow wings for the next seven years. Then we do not need to look for them anywhere but in the sky.

Accompanying my daughter for the last sixteen years has been the greatest joy of my life. The adventures we have shared around the world, and the feeling of comradeship we've developed, are priceless. If you are fortunate enough to have a child in your life, then you need no school of happiness or spiritual retreats. Just watch her/him and learn from them all mysteries about life and how to be. I deeply feel that my daughter and I are only at the beginning of our journey together, and we'll allow our creative expressions to bring harmony and beauty to the world. But before that, here are some pearls of wisdom I've learned during my Voyage to Love for the last five decades on earth:

A simple idea but a complex practice: love yourself and your life will love you too! Did you know that 80% of my students at the Cannes School of Happiness cannot scream loud these three words when I ask them to: "I love myself." Start each day with these magical words and let love be your guide.

Your heart is the gateway between the invisible and the visible, between your dreams and actions. *Get out of your mind and live from the heart*, and you shall never be lost. Do not be afraid that your heart may be broken, hurt, or even shattered into a thousand pieces. A heart breaks again and again until it stays open. And an open heart is your biggest strength, because it will help you to understand yourself better and help light your path.

"Wonder is the beginning of wisdom," said Socrates. *Instead of saying, "I know" start your day, or your sentence, by saying, "I wonder."* Let wonder liberate you from the need to measure yourself, your life, your success, or others. Experience life vertically toward the depths of peace, love, harmony and beauty and act from those depths toward the outer world.

Travel brings power and love back into your life. Set your priorities right and invest in yourself. External gadgets, a new smart phone, or a new bag may look attractive at the beginning, but a plane ticket may change your whole life. Prejudice, self-importance, pride, monotony, and fear all dissipate once you step into another culture or country. Henry Miller said, "One's destination is never a place, but a new way of seeing things." Travel brings that magic into your life.

Say no to any person or any situation that compromises your values, your visions, and who you are. Knowing yourself and what you stand for is the gift you share with the world. No need to feel guilty, obliged, mean, or selfish. Love yourself enough to set boundaries.

It does not rain to make you wet, it just rains. Learn not to take things personally, especially in the matters of the heart (and when you are dealing with the other sex). It is easier to do this when you *take 100% responsibility for yourself.* It does not hurt to use emotional cleansing techniques and go deeper into yourself, but remember your needs determine how you feel about a particular word, deed, action or others.

Limitations, or imposed conditions, or anything that challenges you, are your potential teachers; they push you to be creative. Maya Angelou said, "You may encounter many defeats, but you must not be defeated." Nothing in the world can take the place of knowing why you are pursuing a specific goal and trusting that you shall be guided to the right answers, when you ask right questions.

If you are going to do something, and it is something worth doing, do it wholeheartedly, fully...until the last drop. Whatever moves you and ignites your passion, go after that with all your being. You may fall, but you must learn how to get up after each blow. Don't just get up, but walk, run, and grow your wings, if you have to.

Happiness is something that cannot be taken away from you. If someone or something takes your happiness away, then it was not "real." It was only an illusion of happiness. The true source of happiness is inside of you.

Where there is light, remember there are shadows just around the corner. Accept the reality of what is, and you will step out of illusions faster and find solutions quicker to your life's issues. Khalil Gibran said, "The deeper the sorrow carves into your being, the more joy you can hold." Sorrow and joy, light and shadow, love and hate are but Janus coins of the same reality.

Connection is what we crave most, and we crave what we perceive to be missing from our lives. Connection to other human beings, other living beings, and our surroundings is what makes us human. Connecting with nature is the fastest way to recharge your body, mind, and soul.

Unity is the underlying principle of life. Unity is the inner nature of every soul and the only purpose of life; our mind is the separator and our heart is the connector. What you do is just an extension of who you really are. In life, and in love, there is no you and I. We are all one.

Life is simple, straightforward, fair, and fun. If you are able to connect the dots and solve the puzzle of your own life, you shall live the life you are meant to live...be the person you are meant to be...achieve success in your personal and professional lives. How do you connect the dots? *Practice silence and make time for meditation* and your path will open before your eyes.

How you define yourself defines you. When I was a little girl, my parents insisted that I attend a religious summer school. My teacher defined me as a "girl" and thus directed me to the back of the mosque. I knew I was more than just a girl. I never bought into that limiting definition of myself. I got on with my life and always expanding the definition of who I was: Ivy League professor, United Nations expert, mother, wife, lover, yogini, Cannes School of Happiness founder and, more recently, poetess of the heart, soul doctor, Best-Selling Author®...and I am barely half way into my life. Change and expansion are two facts of life: welcome them with open arms each day.

When you share your gifts without the concern of monetary gains or status, you receive your heart's desires. After university, I asked my parents to send me abroad to learn English better so that I could open my own business in Turkey. It did not happen.

Instead, I searched for alternative ways, and I found that I could live and work in England as a community service volunteer. I left home to be a volunteer in a women's shelter. I discovered the world of volunteering. From that moment onward, every new move or every new job I received started with me as a volunteer, including my dream job at the United Nations as a gender expert.

The road less travelled often leads to unexpected rewards and joy for you and possibly for your love circle too. Do not be tempted by easy paths. Fulfilling your mission in life may be hard, and may even seem daunting at times. If it were easy, everyone would do it. You have the most important ingredient for success in life within and without: passion fueled by dedication, discipline, and a desire to serve humanity. Practice delayed gratification as often as you can and watch love, beauty, and harmony unfold into your life.

Extend your time frame when making important decisions; if you shall not remember it in ten, twenty, thirty, or forty years, then it is not important. Years ago while living in Central Asian villages, I had to cancel my plan of celebrating my fortieth birthday in India, because our engineer had quit the job. I was disappointed. As my birthday approached, I felt myself getting depressed. I could not leave the country and the villagers who had put all their trust in us to bring them safe drinking water. Then, one day, I asked myself one crucial question, "When I am 80, forty years from now on, what shall I remember?" The engineer? His name? Or my miserable fortieth birthday at home? The decision was clear, I made a compromise: travel to Thailand for three days, instead of the two-week retreat in India. As a result of that decision, I discovered my favorite country on earth, my spiritual home, and the placed where I feel effortlessly at peace each time I am in the land of smiles.

Never ever give up your dreams...live them. Dreams help you overcome your limitations, fears, and externally dictated notions of what is achievable or suitable for you. *Only you* know how to harmonize yourself with the music coming from the depths of your soul. Dance with it, sing with it, and dream with it. You are the composer of your own life.

In life, there will always be a gap between what you expect and what you find. See the gap and accept it. But also seek the gift in the gap, in people, and in all of your life's circumstances.

There is no such thing as the right person or the right lover, or even the right relationship. There exists only "right action." Action, made with love from your inner heart, will bring you where you need to be and lead you to the person with whom you shall share your path. No need to search for a lover when you can be the Love.

As long as you are on earth, you are a "work in progress," as is everyone else. You can always change the course of your life and you can always improve. And most importantly, you can always forgive and live your life in freedom.

Pimples come and go: your beauty is eternal. When you focus your attention on your transitory imperfections, you lose your energy unnecessarily. Instead, stay connected to your essence made of love, beauty, and harmony.

Life is always better with dark chocolate! I think, my dear daughter, I do not need to convince you on this. As everything else in life, try it for yourself and decide. Enjoy.

CHAPTER 8

KOLAY GELSIN: MAY IT COME EASY

A SPIRITUAL TURKISH JOURNEY

BY YODY TORRES

I didn't expect to fall in love with a foreign land that held parts of me—my soul, my heart.

At least, not until I went to Turkey for first time in August 2015.

Unexpectedly, my soul fully awakened and I felt connected to this land. I wanted more.

Once I returned to the United States, where I lived, I immediately began looking for ways to return—or at least feel connected—to Turkey. I took language classes and even worked with a Turkish lawyer, just so I could be around their community.

Though I love my homeland, Paraguay, I never felt the yearning for it that I did for Turkey. All I know is that Turkey felt like home…a place of familiarity, a place where I could be me. Even my mother said she never saw me smile the way I smiled in Izmir.

While I ached to go back to the place that felt more like home than anywhere else, I was tied to a small two-bedroom house I owned in a low-income neighborhood in Miami.

I'd bought this house a few years earlier. Attached to it were all my beliefs about what it meant to be a good daughter, good mother, and good sister. The house was my success after a failed marriage. I wanted to prove wrong all the naysayers who told me that a single woman, alone, could not buy a house. And I did; but the truth is, I was looking to prove more than that. I wanted to prove my worth to others. I sought, in particular, my family's approval. Even more deeply than that, my inner child yearned for parental consent to be an adult.

What better way to become an adult than buy a house?

Yet, there were challenges maintaining this tiny home that should not have been difficult. Multiple problems kept rising until it was clear I had to sell the house—or lose it.

It was time to face my illusions and let go of the emotional investments and attachments I had in this home. I had to begin seeing that my worth and identity were not determined by anything outside of myself—not even home ownership or what others thought. In order to connect to myself, I had to lose the house and my identity.

The little Miami house sold in December 2016. I knew that while the egoic part of myself still wanted the Miami house, my spirit needed the freedom to truly reconnect with what brings me wholeness. The sale freed all the outmoded attachments and stories I told myself and allowed me to travel internationally for a year.

I've always loved traveling. It helps me take on new perspectives, question my belief patterns, and identify long neglected desires or pain, buried deep within—but with a sense of ease and grace instead of resistance. Something about being in different places requires fluidity and inspires a sense of rapture and bliss.

By the fall of 2017, I travelled to eight different countries, including my place of birth Paraguay. Even after fitting in two trips to Turkey, it still called to me, wanting more of my heart, more of my soul. More healing. More connection.

Izmir—located in the Aegean Region of Turkey, formerly known as Smyrna—especially called me loudly. For Christians, this is the land of the "Seven Churches" and the "House of Virgin Mary." For pagans, it's the land of Goddesses. I decided I wanted to move there. It spoke to the alchemy of my Catholic upbringing and my current spirituality. I was ready for a rebirth and to be reconnected with my Soul Home. Our souls are not always attached to our place of birth: Belonging and wholeness may be found elsewhere.

As serendipity would have it, in the month of death (October), on the first day in Scorpio—known as the stage of transformation—I arrived back to Izmir, Turkey. With its three million people, Izmir is the most westernized city in Turkey. Though I felt safe there, even traveling alone as a single woman, I decided it was wise to find a hotel in a popular tourist area and take time to decide where I wanted to live. After working as a traveling nanny for seven years, sleeping in three-to-four different places each week, I wanted to finally lay my head on the same pillow—for at least 30 days!

To keep connected and help my family know I was safe, I turned on my iPhone's "Find and Share Your Location." That enabled my sister to check on me whenever I had a Wi-Fi signal. This way, she could identify my whereabouts and know I was well. My family had voiced their concerns about me traveling to Turkey—especially solo!

As I walked around Izmir, I was in a constant state of awe, discovering history everywhere I turned: the Bazaar, antique marketplaces, historic Smyrna. I wandered the streets of the tourist area, Konak, without a map or cell service. I was free and in a childlike sense of wonder and euphoria. I took in the pier and marina, explored restaurants, and conversed with locals, who were patient with my lack of Turkish language skills. I fell in love with everything. I was home.

While I've seen many sunsets in my life, even in exotic places, I had never experienced them anything close to like I did in Izmir. The sun kissed the sky as if in ritual...maybe it was the energy of Artemis in the hills of Ephesus.

My love affair continued. The more I surrendered to Turkey, the more I craved her. I found an Airbnb with a single room and private bathroom in the Bostanli area of the Karsiyaka district. I was enchanted. As a former New Yorker, Miami resident, and small town girl from Paraguay, Bostanli merged the best of all three worlds. The neighborhood is comparable to Soho or Astoria (Queens) New York. It's a family-oriented area with an active nightlife. Even late into the evening, I felt safe wandering the streets.

Travel has its own Muse and it urges you to listen. It asks you to find connections—with the land and others—in order to fully reconnect with yourself. This often means following your intuition and going places you hadn't planned...just to see what kind of magic unfolds. I knew it was part of my soul journey in Turkey to truly listen and not question where my heart took me.

One adventure led me to Erzurum—in the center of Turkey—one of the coldest regions. Knowing I "needed" to meet a writer I found on Instagram who wrote two books about Syrian refugees living in the area, I booked a one-way ticket and didn't bother to check the weather, or the altitude.

Within a few hours, I was shivering in the cold, completely unprepared and without a winter coat, gloves or hat. Suddenly, my severe vertigo kicked in. I recognized it from the high altitude in Aspen, Colorado when I experienced insomnia, heart palpitations, and a burst eardrum, which caused me to almost drive off a hill. I knew I needed to immediately take the first bus out of Erzurum—and certainly not a plane!—to alleviate my altitude sickness. Despite this, I knew that the connection with this man's writing was important and I was taken by the depth of his sense of social responsibility and openness to share (even with a language barrier), he didn't hesitate to try to show me the most that he could of his hometown.

Later, I felt guided to an area in southeastern Turkey called Urfa, not far from the Euphrates River. In ancient times it was known as Edessa, and is the alleged birthplace of Abraham. Being highly sensitive and intuitive, as I walked around this multi-ethnic place holding sacred sites for many religions, I could feel it ALL: burned churches, the synagogues, sun-moon temples—a collision of belief systems underneath every call for prayer.

In Harran, just a little south of Urfa, I stayed in a 300-year-old beehive house maintained by the same family lineage. During my four days there, I observed women cooking, cleaning, and serving food and tea for the men in the house. Feeling a sense of sisterhood, one evening, I convinced them to let me give them a facial treatment, since they kept complimenting me on my skin. In my native Guarani language from Paraguay, *pire-pora* means "good mood, healthy happiness" or literally "good, healthy skin." I believe our soul constantly transforms, just like our skin; skin is an indicator of our well-being. I wanted to take a few moments to make these women—sisters of my soul—feel special and cared for, since they were always caring for others, first. It felt like a healing moment for all of us.

Many people warned me against going to Turkey. They said it wasn't safe, it was too unstable...and with all the political upheaval and war in Syria, that it wasn't wise, especially for a woman to travel there alone. Yet, I chose to listen to my heart and travel even further into southeastern Turkey, near the Tigris River, on a route that connects to Syria and Iraq.

I reached Mardin; the historic city overlooking limestone plateaus. Its honey-colored stone buildings seeped into my soul, just like the scent of sumac that was so readily in the air as I walked down the ancient sidewalks. I didn't want to go inside the buildings. Instead, I stood outside, admiring their design, shape, and history. It's as if I glimpsed into all the civilizations that had been here, and I felt that with each step I took. I felt the energy alive with a soothing breeze that felt like home. I shed more of my skin—more of my unwanted attachments and old identities—revealing more of my soul to myself.

Each time I listened to where I was meant to travel, I'd meet a lovely person who blessed me with their presence. In Mardin, I met a Taiwanese woman, also traveling solo, en route to Dara, an ancient Mesopotamian ruin—only five miles from the Syrian border, that's rarely spoken about in tourist circles—to bury a letter from her boyfriend. Together, we traveled there…and I felt a sense of joy and hope emanating from it, witnessing love full of hope.

I've visited many sacred places in the world, seeking the place my soul longed for and belonged. I found it in Turkey: my Soul Home.

The unique experience of traveling, led by my feminine intuition, took me on a journey of saving myself, of coming to a place of belonging for me. From this place within my heart, I now feel complete and celebrate the Divine Grace that whispers to us new possibilities, even when it takes challenges and a "falling away" to experience it…like losing my old, egoic attachments and identities wrapped into a little house in Miami. The world is larger than this. Our souls are larger than any attachment.

I want all sensitive women to feel inspired to travel and follow their hearts—especially when it doesn't "make sense."

You just might find exactly where you belong: To yourself.

Kolay gelsin: may it come easy.

About Yody

Born an old soul, from her early childhood, Yody Torres felt an inner knowing and connection to the subtle world, beyond what her eyes could see and her mind could explain. Her goal was to become a nun, travel the world, help children, and write about it.

This journey took her from her native Guarani land in Paraguay to Argentina. There she became an Aspirant with The Sisters of St. Paul, a religious Catholic organization dedicated to produce and publish videos, books, and audio material around the world. Also using all kinds of social media, Yody truly believes that St. Paul was one of the first instagram influencers of his time.

Life, just like a modern day GPS navigation system, gave her dreams and plans with plenty of re-routes, taking her from Buenos Aires, Argentina to New York City in 1999. From a Nun aspirant, Yody was married with a child by 2001, and then moved to Miami in 2008. Her family obligations took her away from her spiritual commitment. Through a catalytic divorce, and family traumas, she discovered her inner yearning with Reiki Energy work and a deeply healing "solo" trip to Turkey in 2015.

Yody considers herself an emergency room kind of soul reader, and she likes reading and studying about all kinds of spirituality practices; including Tarot, Oracle Cards and different religious practices. She integrate into her counseling the lessons she's learned from all kinds of jobs she's held in the past. This includes, but is not limited to a car wash attendant, Social Media Manager, Immigration paperwork translator, nanny, Special Education, Childcare, and in her darkest days, she found relief in volunteering for organizations sheltering and rehabilitating young woman and mentoring youth transitioning out Foster Care in a low income neighborhood in Miami.

Yody prides herself in always respecting her client's core belief systems and their identity while keeping an honest sharing ground. She currently works with clients from all walks of life, including attornies, international producers, DJs, make up artists and corporate executives. Some of her former clients considered meeting her as their catalyst: not a smooth ride, mainly a burst of creative energy. She compares her work to that of an ambulance driver, her work is hardly ever noticed, nor her name announced, but she always answers a 911 call (by the Universe, God, angels, spirit) to be right where she needs to be.

Yody considers traveling solo and visiting Turkey her way to renew and recharge her physical energy. She is currently working on a children's book with one of her kids, and setting up an online store with her sister to sell products from her travels.

If you feel the need to call 911 for your soul with a one on one session, or you want to peek at Yody's new hobbies and travels, you can visit:

www.yodymarlen.com
Instagram: @YodyMarlen & @GreenSolyLuna
Facebook: Spirituality305style

CHAPTER 9

UNEXPECTED ROAD

BY CHRISTINE ROSSI-FLAMAND

Lounging in a deck chair in the sun, Rose let her mind wander as she listened to R.E.M.'s latest hit, birds chirping in the background. Agentle warmth caressed her face, while her cat, Pepper, jumped up and laid on her belly. Images of her past came back to her in fragments. What a tortuous and obstacle-strewn journey! After a childhood shattered by the divorce of her parents, leaving her alone with an alcoholic mother and deprived of fatherly love, Rose, a rebellious teenager with low self-esteem, had started frequenting alternative venues. She had experimented with all sorts of, more or less, illegal substances. A short respite had followed. After obtaining a business degree, she had worked as a teller in a major Swiss bank. Yet, in these times of crisis, unemployment had hit her hard. Not once, but after she had finally been hired again by another bank, it had struck again. In debt, Rose had to pick up odd jobs here and there to make ends meet. Thankfully, her exuberant Granny was at her side as ever, always generous towards her only granddaughter, lifting her spirits and dropping a few pennies into her purse whenever she visited.

Rose had met Marc on a drunken night out at a bar. Oh Marc! She'd fallen head over heels for the hunk. Turning a deaf ear to her friend's disapproving comments, she'd given in completely to the advances of this serial lady-killer, a tormented soul and recovering heroin addict with a mercurial disposition. He had preyed on Rose's unconditional love and emotional dependency to impose himself psychologically, gradually forcing her into submission, making her almost invisible. One day, she'd had enough. She left Marc. She took her fate back into her own hands, reconnected with her friends, and took up sports again. Now, in her deck chair, Rose realized all her efforts were finally paying off. Indeed! After fighting to prove her worth as a temp, the young woman had just landed a fixed contract in a prestigious bank. Yes, she could be proud of herself, she asserted to an incredulous Pepper.

The phone jolted her out of her daydreaming.

"Hey, it's Frank! So, are we going out to celebrate your new job as planned? Japanese joint before we hit the town?"

"For sure! Let's party!" enthused Rose, "Come over at 7 for drinks?"

"Sounds good babe!" replied her old pal, and partner in crime on her wildest nights, before hanging up.

She glanced at her watch and thought, "It's only 3, just enough time to ride up Mount Salève and back."

Rose hopped onto her bike and took off toward the mountain. As she pedaled, she started thinking about Marc. In her heart, she still hoped he might change and finally come to understand that they're meant for each other and, who knows, regret all the harm he did to her. Would he change though? Deep down, she didn't really believe so. Her thoughts turned to the evening ahead. As usual, she'd be a little late, and Frank would already be standing by the door with a bottle of champagne. Of course, she'd make him wait while she took a shower, slipped on a sexy skirt and quickly brushed on a little makeup. No matter: They'd gorge on sushi, party all night in the trendiest clubs, and meet loads of, more or less, savory characters. The next day would probably follow along the same lines with a brunch at the bathhouse, followed by the usual Sunday afternoon drinks that extend too long into the evening. Sure, she wouldn't be particularly fresh-faced for her meeting Monday morning, but after all, you only live once, right?

When Rose became aware of the car speeding toward her it was already too late. The Fiat Dino hit her head-on and sent her flying 80 feet. Her condition was so bad she had to be flown to hospital by helicopter. She went through a battery of tests, and the bad news started pouring in as the results arrive: severe head trauma, lesion to the right temporal lobe, multiple cerebral contusions, leg broken in three places, bruising on the whole body.

The words fell like bombs on Rose's bright future, although she isn't even aware of it yet. She is floating in a thick mist. How long did it last? She didn't really know. Her first clear and precise memory is that of her father, standing at the foot of her bed, wearing an unusual outfit and looking at her crestfallen before sighing and leaving the room, obviously distraught. Where is she? Aside from her close family, the people around her are all strangers, albeit attentive, even empathetic. Gradually, Rose began to understand that she is in intensive care at the hospital, where visits are strictly limited.

Within two weeks, Rose's condition stabilizes and she is transferred to a private unit in the hospital where the pace is altogether different. Nurses are required to adhere to a strict schedule. At 6:30, the nurse's aide enters the room, curt and mechanical, turning on the neon light and pulling up the blinds. To Rose, all light feels blinding, all noise is like an assault. Her heartbeat starts racing. Nevertheless, Rose has no choice but to submit to the schedule. Shower at 6:45. Breakfast at 7:15. At 9:30, the doctors confer around her bed. Lunch is at 11:30, with dinner at 6:00 pm sharp. She remains apathetic to this frenetic pace and to the medical staff's discussions. All she knows is that she is suffering from a terrible headache and a permanently overwhelming fatigue. Days go by like this, away from banks, friends, Marc and Japanese joints.

One day at noon, Rose's stepmom visits her. Susanne married her father 15 years ago, but until now they've never really connected. The young woman complains, "Meals are bland here, they have no taste."

Susanne tries the food, "It smells good, and it's nicely seasoned. Really, it's quite tasty, especially for a public hospital."

Rose insists, "It's absolutely tasteless!"

Susanne tries it again, unconvinced, but she'd rather change the topic, sensing her step-daughter's frayed nerves. When she leaves the room, she seeks out the head doctor and quickly tells him about the episode.

He replies offhandedly, "We'll do some tests. Lack of smell, or *anosmia*, and taste, *ageusia*, can occur following severe brain injuries."

Unfortunately, the results are unequivocal: Both senses are truly gone. Henceforth, her world will be devoid of fragrances and savors. Rose hardly eats anymore; she becomes weaker and thinner by the day.

Three weeks go by in this gloomy atmosphere until she is admitted to a private clinic for a period of "convalescence," as the doctors call it, with a slightly premature sense of optimism. A plush room awaits her with an amazing view over Lake Geneva and the surrounding mountains. It's beautiful and relaxing. Upon arrival, the nurse's aide brings her a thermos full of hot tea and a snack. The very attentive hospital staff helps her settle in.

"What am I doing here? Where is my life?" Rose asks. She doesn't understand. Total confusion; things are in shambles in her mind, and her head hurts, as if it was caught in a vise. Dinner is served in her room on a platter with a little tablecloth and a flower for decoration. The nurse's aide lifts the cloche, revealing a platter of fish with green vegetables and some rice. There's also some cheese and dessert, but Rose isn't hungry. The sight of food makes her nauseous. Tired, she lies down and falls asleep.

When she wakes up, darkness has filled the room except for a glimmer of light under the door. She feels a little calmer. Where exactly is she? Oh, yes, at the clinic. Her dinner has been replaced with herbal tea. She sits up in her bed and pours herself a cup. The half-light in the room is pleasant. Minutes go by. She looks out the window and tries to evaluate the situation. Although the events have all been explained to her, she struggles to understand why she is here. She barely has any recollection of her hospital stay. Her broken leg is in a cast, that's clear. The anosmia and ageusia, the ringing in the ears, the headaches, the fatigue, and the physical pain associated with the shock, those too are clear. But, the rest of it?

Rose can't think straight anymore, she struggles to recall what she's just been told. Days go by and they all feel the same. The smallest sound startles her and she constantly feels threatened, making her irritable and bad-tempered. Her daily life is interspersed with various therapy sessions with the occasional visit by her friends and family, all of whom are truly concerned by her condition. What future prospects does the young woman have left?

Six weeks later, it's time for Rose to leave this protected environment and return to her apartment. Rose is anxious: "Other people have moved on with their life, while mine has stopped dead. How will I deal with my return to reality?" Her father comes to pick her up and drive her home. As she opens the door, she's welcomed by Pepper's disdainful meowing. A flood of happy memories from her previous life resurface. Her mother has filled the fridge, prepared several meals, and even left a bunch of flowers on the table. She's overwhelmed with emotion and bursts into tears.

After a few days, a routine sets in. Rose continues outpatient treatment: physiotherapy, ergotherapy, and psychotherapy. Patiently, through her rehabilitation sessions, she fights to regain control of her legs and daily activities, and to deal with her new living conditions. Nevertheless, depression and anxiety settle deep into her existence. The harsh and bleak winter further amplifies her angst.

In the early days of spring, Rose finally manages, after months of efforts, to walk almost normally again. The icing on the cake: Her beloved Granny is back from her travels and planning to come and see her. Seeing her grandmother's bright face, she is overwhelmed by an emotional tsunami.

"Hello darling, I'm so happy to see you again! How are you?" Granny asks as she gives her a long, warm hug.

After listening to Rose, Granny suggests a walk on the shores of the lake. "It'll do you good to get out of here and to see the wonderful flowers!"

"Why not?" says Rose, still rattled by spasms. It's a pleasant walk; the weather is divine. They stop at the terrace of a small bar and order two teas. Reunited in their close complicity, they engage in a long conversation.

They're interrupted by a male voice calling out, "Hi Rose!" Rose turns around and is surprised to discover Thomas, a schoolmate from high-school, perched on roller-skates.

"Oh, hi Thomas!"

"So, enjoying the sunshine? What have you been up to?" he asks.

Not really knowing why, Rose pours her heart out to this welcome recipient and tells him the whole story: the accident, the hospital, the tests, the diagnostics, the pain, the doctors, but also the lawsuit she has filed against the road hog who shattered her life, and all her daily struggles.

As she explains how her life has turned out, Thomas, dumbstruck and dismayed becomes increasingly more sympathetic. In the end, he gives her his card, "Here, here's my number. Call me and I'll take you on a boat ride if you want. It could help take your mind off things." Rose takes the business card and her leave, thanking him for listening.

"I say, sweetheart, he seems like a nice young man," Granny chirps once he's moved away. "I hope you'll get in touch with him!"

"Maybe," says Rose, without much conviction.

***

Sitting comfortably at the wheel of her BMW, Rose stops to let an unkempt and unsteady looking pedestrian cross. "My God," she thinks to herself, "the poor guy, he looks very young to be in that state."

In the back, two voices call out, "Mum, did you bring snacks?"

"Yes, of course, sweethearts, I've got apples from the garden. Here."

While she's at a halt, she gets the fruit out of her bag. As she lifts her head up, she is shocked to see the pedestrian's face: It's Marc! Their eyes lock briefly. A chill runs down her spine. Seeing his haggard, weary air—although he's suffered no accident, he's just paying the price of his excesses—she realizes how much she fought day after day, month after month, year after year, to regain the life that had been taken from her, to become the woman she is today: strong and committed, a caring mother, a loving and beloved wife.

As she starts off again, the phone rings and a cheerful and familiar voice booms out of the car's loudspeakers:

"Hi honey! How are you? Did you pick up the kids at school?"

"Sure, darling, they're here, we'll be home in 15 minutes."

"Oh great! By the way, I got the visas. We're all leaving for Japan to celebrate our ten-year anniversary!"

"Wow, great news! I'm so lucky to have a husband like you!"

"But... I love you, Rose."

"I love you too, Thomas."

About Christine

Christine Rossi-Flamand's hopes of a brilliant career in banking were dashed in the blink of an eye when she was just 26. Strong-willed and determined, she walked away from the ordeal stronger than ever, becoming involved in causes dear to her heart. Her journey inspired her to take up writing, and she is currently working on her first book.

A lovely young Swiss girl, intelligent and outgoing, she lived a charmed life: a good education, fluency in three languages, a well-regarded degree, a job in a major Swiss bank, and a busy social life. But fate intervened when she was hit by a car on a beautiful summer afternoon. Quickly declared unable to return to her professional endeavors, she channeled all her energy, creativity, and leadership into promoting the values most dear to her: respect for others, environmental protection, nutrition and health awareness.

Her unwavering commitment and perseverance, combined with her outstanding organizational abilities and her unremitting desire to help, turned her into a key member of JCI Geneva (JCI is an international federation of volunteers involving some 200,000 active young citizens). There she headed several working committees related to various issues such as children, nature, and education. She took on roles successively welcoming new members, as webmaster, general secretary, instructor, and president. Wearing all these different hats helped her acquire skills in new areas and participate in community partnership programs and in conferences where she met people from all walks of life, yet all driven by the same passion. Christine was awarded the title of JCI Senator, an international and lifetime honor.

Deprived of the senses of taste and smell since her accident, Christine overcame her disability, even becoming an accomplished chef. Every day she delights her family and friends with her cooking, using only fresh seasonal ingredients. A cake recipe that she developed was even commercialized on a local scale. In parallel, she has kept the books for a wood working business, digitizing the accounting system and updating a number of administrative procedures. Finally, she has developed her artistic side by practicing photography semi-professionally and in her family life, where she seizes every opportunity to handcraft original objects.

Today, Christine is the mother of two children, to whom she strives to transmit the good education she received, fully aware of how important this learning is to understanding proper behavior and to being at ease in all circumstances. Always full of initiative and keen to take up new challenges, Christine started writing her first book several months ago and is passionate about this new activity, while remaining fully engaged in her existing commitments.

You can reach Christine at:

unexpectedroad@bluewin.ch
christinef_@hotmail.com

CHAPTER 10

ONE-WAY TICKET

BY LAURA DE WAAL

To work, but not let go of one's wandering spirit.
To view the world as new, each and every day,
But not lose your place, your roots.
Live, experience life, fulfill your appetite,
Find your tree with many rings.

This is an excerpt from a poem I wrote at the age of 16. Twenty years have passed since then, and happily one of the aspects of the work I have chosen allows my nomadic spirit to be fulfilled. I have a vegan handbag line that allows me to work with artisans from around the world to support and strengthen disadvantaged communities with fair trade or higher wages.

One of these work related adventures was my first time to Laos. I found myself travelling from Bangkok, in the midst of a heavy rainstorm in a propeller plane, to land in Luang Prabang, the second largest city in Laos. The rain had subsided as I stepped off of the plane and I was hit with a burst of humidity and heat. This was at the end of Laos' rainy season and I had entered what felt like a jungle, surrounded by palm trees and tropical plants. I left the airport for the city center in the back of a motorcycle converted to a Tuk Tuk with a heavy gasoline smell. Once it picked up a little speed, I had the wind on my face and it was shortly accompanied by a big smile, as I immediately fell in love with Luang Prabang. Buddhist Monks still stroll the streets, in their unmistakable saffron colored robes, amongst the numerous temples throughout the city. The architecture is beautiful and there are many well preserved French Colonial buildings with wooden shutters and wrap around balconies, now converted into guesthouses and restaurants. I had the next two days, in this beautiful city, to find a driver to take me the eight hours southeast toward my reason for coming to this magical country.

In my search for a driver, I received many warnings that the drive would be long and winding through mountain roads. Recommendations of carrying sick bags as well as wearing a long skirt for the journey, in case a bathroom stop is needed with no toilet to be found, made me a little anxious of the upcoming journey. Despite the warnings, I found a driver who spoke some English for my drive south through the zigzagging unpaved roads. Our route through the mountains was breathtaking, literally and physically. The landscape of Laos is beautiful and peaceful looking, despite its dark past. We drove by steep cliffs and incredible look out points coupled with small villages and huts. Many of the small houses would have hundreds of bright red chili peppers spread out drying across rooftops and spilling out of baskets. The roads were always lined with chickens and puppies amidst walking locals and school children that always seemed to have smiles on their faces. After eight hours of traveling, I had arrived to a small town near the Plain of Jars in Phonsavan, Laos.

Phonsavan primarily consists of one small main street with a few cafes and shops. Many of which have huge missiles and bombshells turned into decorations, and sometimes they are even being used as pillars. Laos was heavily bombed during the Vietnam War and remains the most heavily bombed country per capita in history to date. It is estimated that the U.S. dropped an equivalent to a planeload of bombs every eight minutes, 24-hours a day from 1964 to 1973 on Laos. These bombings, known as the Secret War, destroyed villages and displaced hundreds of thousands of Lao civilians. To make matters worse, close to a third of the bombs did not explode, leaving the land contaminated with unexploded ordnance (UXO), even today. Much of the countryside that could be farmland contains these UXOs making it very dangerous for the Lao people to cultivate their own land. The cluster bombs, which are now partly buried in the ground, are sometimes discovered by children thinking they are round yellow balls, when they go to pick them up they are tragically harmed or even killed. While there are efforts being made to clear the UXOs, the progress is slow and statistically a person is still killed almost every day by these bombs.

This area of Lao is one of the most impacted provinces by the Secret War and some of the locals here became creative with the abundance of scrap metal fragments of bombs they found. These Lao artisans started to melt the aluminum down into spoons and then into small souvenirs to provide some additional financial income on top of their farming. With the ingenuity of these artisans, by repurposing this metal, they have turned a negative element into a positive. I was really exited by what they were doing and wanted to help support their ingenuity and have them create the hardware for my handbags. I immediately began to do research on how to ethically and safely work with these artisans. As they are dealing with UXOs in some scenarios I wanted to be sure that if I were to work with them I would not end up doing more harm than good. Therefore, I found and contacted a non-profit agency that had been helping to train the artisans on how to safely distinguish which metal was safe to use and touch. This metal is also only handled and worked with by adults. Through the organization, I was put into contact with Somechit, the head artisan from the community I was planning to work with.

One of the things I learned after starting my own company is that nothing happens overnight, so you shouldn't wait too long to get things started. Learning as you grow your business will happen no matter how prepared you may think you are. A business plan and setting up goals and principles for your company or brand are important as they will keep you on course, however sometimes you just have to hold your breath and jump right in. Throughout my twenties, I shuffled back and forth between the design retail world and working for non-profits. For me it was important to somehow also bring my passion for helping others (people and animals) into my brand. I still have a lot of goals of how I want that to take place, but first I knew I did not want to harm animals in creating my products. Next I wanted to employ and work with artisans whenever possible in creating my handbags. Ultimately, I want to create beautiful modern handbags that have a positive impact on the people creating them and a positive energy for the people buying them. Being in Laos was one of those moments for me, I didn't exactly know where I was going or who I was meeting, but I was exited about the possibilities and I jumped right in.

There are only two days in the year that nothing can be done.
One is called Yesterday and the other is called Tomorrow.
Today is the right day to love, believe, do and mostly live.
- Dalai Lama XIV

Finally the day I would get to meet with Somechit arrived. I had only spoken to Somechit via phone calls and a text-messaging program. The only image I had of him was a photograph of him in a well-pressed uniform. I had assumed this was some sort of military uniform. Later I learned that this uniform was one that teachers wear in Lao. The address I had was only his name and his village; I had mailed him a package with this same 'address' and it had taken over six months to reach him. It had been a long process to get to the stage we were now, and I was very excited to finally be meeting the artisans.

We set out to find Somechit and the other artisans that belonged to what has become known as the "spoon village" due to the spoons they have been creating from the melted bomb scrap metal. The drive led to an unpaved, bumpy, dirt road that cut through bright green, empty plains of grass. We were forced to drive slowly as the van hurdled through rocks and pockets of mud. I saw a small sign sticking in the grass next to our van; it's a warning sign from MAG, an international organization dedicated to locating and clearing unexploded bombs and landmines in affected areas. The writing on the sign is written in Laotian, but is clearly warning that a bomb disposal team is in the area and to not walk in that direction. A large blast echoed from close by, with the sight of smoke rising into the clouds. This is not an unusual day for the locals living here, as these bombs are a part of their lives and landscape.

My driver, Sitdao, and new friend for the journey, rolls down the window as we pull next to a teenage boy to ask if he knew the village we were looking for. None of the streets are named or marked and the homes do not have number addresses, but he points us in the right direction and says he believes we are about two villages away. As we continued driving we approach a small school and community of homes right along the road, with livestock and chickens roaming about aimlessly. Across from the school we notice three people looking and smiling at us, as we get closer I recognize that among them is Somechit. We were greeted by him along with his wife and brother in-law and are given a tour of Somechit's home and his outdoor kiln where he melts the metal.

I was invited to join Somechit and his family for lunch. I was told that his sister, Diptee, was the best cook in the family and she did not disappoint. She created several traditional Lao dishes as well as a vegan spicy soup for me. Everything was eaten by hand (including the rice) with the exception of the soup, which I ate with one of their handcrafted bomb metal spoons. We gathered in their home around a table as her young son napped effortlessly on the floor near us. After a few hours of conversation and good food we felt as though we were all old friends. My father's side of the family is Dutch and we have a word in Dutch "gezellig," which does not have a direct translation in English, but one explanation is the comfortable and happy feeling you have when you are with friends or family. Sometimes you can substitute it with the word "cozy." As I gathered with Somechit and his family in his home it felt very "gezellig." As is often tradition in Lao gatherings, we all shared one glass to drink the local Beerlao Lager. This beer is a favorite among backpackers and locals alike in Laos. Beer drinking is done similar to a shot, however each person drinks in turn. The beer is poured in the glass and you drink the beer in one big sip before passing the glass onto the next person and this continues until everyone is feeling quite happy.

I spent the next few days getting to know Somechit and the other artisans. I also learned that most worked as farmers and some as teachers as well. Somechit was the English teacher at the local school and I asked to have a visit with the children. The headmaster asked if I could help to create a fundraiser page for the school to raise money for repairs that the school needed. I was happy to be able to help, and I have also dedicated a portion of any of my handbags made with the Laos metal to this school. They need a new roof to keep the local bats from sleeping and defecating in the classrooms, they need updated toilet facilities, and they also want to level out the play yard so that the children can play sports. Luckily the yard had already been cleared and checked by a MAG bomb team for any UXOs. There are several craters left from where bombs were found and detonated, leaving the playground yard safe but not useable for sports. I am excited to see the change that will happen over the next years as I continue to work with the artisans in this village.

When I left Somechit and the artisans, I left happy with having made new friends, the start of a working collaboration and the knowledge that I would be back again. I believe travel and new cultural experiences are some of the best ways to discover more about yourself. It offers the opportunity to meet new people that you would never have had the chance to meet. It is healthy to get out of your routine, and also your comfort zone, and see the world from new perspectives. Seeing how other people and cultures live can really broaden and open your mind to challenge your own assumptions. Often you take back a little piece of each culture to strengthen your own experiences and customs back home. The people of Laos were so welcoming and kindhearted, despite the many current obstacles they face. I truly admire them and the genuine kindness I felt in their eyes.

These interactions and experiences continue to deepen and develop my self-understanding as well as my perception of the world. I often name my designs after women that I find inspiring. It is a small personal nod to them as they are the women who have made me who I am today. In my first collection, I named a bag style after my mother, Jackie. My mother has always been a big part of my support system and she recently found and shared a poem I wrote her before leaving for college. I feel it is still relevant today as I embark on my new company:

The Wind's Reminder

> *Longing for the wind*
> *I search the sky.*
> *A calming existence,*
> *With everything stretched before me.*
> *A breeze catches me*
> *And a realization pulls at me*
> *While the wind teases my hair,*
> *You too, must have once*
> *Longed for more*
> *Searched the skies.*
> *But I confined you*
> *With full stomach,*
> *Yet you engulfed the responsibility of me.*
> *You enveloped me in love.*
> *You've always had*
> *An amorous*
> *Altruistic presence.*
> *You've sheltered me*

Held me safely
Yet let me wander.
Encouraged
To have my own identity,
Become independent
Away from your sheltered embrace
Yet still safe, protected
And loved.
You let me know
I could make my own life,
My own choices,
But your arms would always be open.
The wind is picking up
And the leaves create
Their own hurricane.
Circling, hurrying
Racing
Calling me.
Though the wind
May carry me,
Your arms will always
Take me home.

Don't be afraid to get swept up and to take that leap to do something you have wanted to do. For me it was staying true to my ideals when starting my company, VEGGANI. I knew certain things would be paramount: no animals harmed, a positive impact on people, and make steps towards doing as little damage to the environment as possible.

On my trip leaving Somechit I was caught in a mudslide and had to wait until the roads were cleared and safe again for travel. This meant I was waiting on the side of the road with locals, other travellers, and even a pair of goats. Soon, though, I was in the back of a pick up truck sitting on a sun-bleached rug, for cushioning, with the wind once again in my hair and a new adventure to inspire my soul. Life is a one-way ticket where the destination should never be the goal. Make sure you enjoy this journey.

About Laura

Laura de Waal is a designer who works from her heart. She has a passion for animal welfare that influences her personal and professional lives: she is an adopted animal parent, a vegan, and she only uses vegan materials in her designs. Laura is an entrepreneur, designer, feminist, author, humanitarian, travel enthusiast, bisexual, LGBTQ ally, artist, and animal rights supporter.

Laura also has a passion of working to support under-privileged women and children. Today, she has incorporated that vital mission into her business as well. Laura's passion for philanthropy began in her youth. In her late teens, Laura taught an art class for blind and special needs children. Then, in college, she co-taught an afterschool Art program for underprivileged elementary and middle school students. Laura also volunteered with a dog rescue while in college, fostering and finding homes for abandoned dogs. Laura has a BFA from The School of the Museum of Fine Arts at Tufts University in Boston, where she studied Fine Art and Gender Studies.

In her twenties, Laura focused on fine art and has shared her work in several galleries and universities. She became the tour booker and a member of Leslie and the Lys, an art centric all female performance band that toured the US and Europe. The band was showcased on MTV's *TRL show, Yo Gabba Gabba, The Dr. Demento* radio show, *Tom Green's House Tonight* show and the VH1 network, to name a few. Laura left the band after several years to work in the retail world. She worked her way from Product Development Intern to Assistant Buyer to Design Assistant for a women's clothing brand. Later, she designed children's clothing and accessories for another brand.

Laura felt something was missing from her work and returned again to the non-profit world. She worked in Philadelphia as an executive assistant for a program whose mission was to provide a supportive and safe space via after school programs and a summer camp for children of non-traditional families, mostly in the LGBTQ community. Working back and forth between the non-profit and retail world, Laura wanted to combine her passions and embrace her creative spirit by founding and creating her own company and brand that would promote her ethics.

Laura de Waal is the founder of Conscientious Trends and the designer behind VEGGANI handbags. VEGGANI is a vegan handbag brand that believes in the protection of people, animals, and the planet. VEGGANI works with and empowers artisans, while also incorporating recycled materials into the designs whenever possible. All VEGGANI products are always made from cruelty-free, vegan materials.

Laura was born in Switzerland to an American mother and a Dutch father. Much of her childhood was spent in Belgium, with summers spent in Alabama. Today, she lives with her fiancée and their adopted dog in Philadelphia.

Visit www.veggani.com to see Laura's designs and some of the artisans that she is currently working with.

You can reach out to Laura at Laura@veggani.com

CHAPTER 11

WHY TRAVEL IS THE BEST MEDICINE TO HEAL A BROKEN HEART?

BY BILLUR SUU

I purchased an around-the-world ticket two years ago, and that ticket changed my whole life. In fifty days, not only did I heal my broken heart, but I also gave birth to myself. I am convinced that solo travel is the best medicine for a woman to heal a broken relationship. Why?

During travel, we shift our focus from our loved ones to whatever captures our attention: nature; new, exotic, and strange things; or people. Travel easily diverts us from an ever-inquisitive and even obsessive mind. You become absorbed by a new place or culture. Or, if you are like me, you get up early every morning to see the sunrise, capturing the essence of the new place at the dawn of a new day. Without realizing it, you start taking in the new environment, people, or culture, and you let them fill you up. Then one moment arrives, I call it "the moment of travel magic," and you are full, whole, and complete. You live in the moment. If darkness is simply the absence of light, you have no place anymore for the troubles, problems, or challenges of your daily life.

After that magical moment of being filled up by nature, you easily turn your awareness to yourself, to your inner heart and your inner voice. You define yourself in relation to nature and realize how small you are, and how small your problems are. You feel, see, touch, accept, love, cherish, and finally define yourself in this new energy.

This is exactly what happened to me in fifty days. I had no one to feed, make happy, satisfy, or entertain except myself. I started noticing my body parts. First taking the time to look at them, then allowing my feet to play with the rain or the wind or rest under the blazing sun. And most importantly, I got out of my mind and let my heart guide me.

Out of all the countries I travelled or lived in, Machu Picchu holds a special place in my heart. I was gifted with a magical encounter, a spiritual renewal, and a new way of being that I did not expect at all. When I was waiting to accommodate myself with the high altitude in Cusco before spending the day in Machu Picchu, I had the urge to write a letter to my beloved describing how I saw the healing path for us.

"It is a simple four-step process envisioned by my left brain. First, we both go back to the past year and recall what debris or hurts have stayed in our memory. Without blocking or judging, we write them down one by one. This could be a word, an action, or a behavior. In the second step, we share all the negative feelings that were created in each of us due to those words, actions, or behaviors. Then we replace those particular negative memories with a positive one. This could be done either in writing or in a heart-sharing session face-to-face. That positive action could be sharing one lesson we learned, creating a new vision, or making a commitment. In the fourth step, we write each other an appreciation and thank-you letter for choosing to heal ourselves and each other, and for displaying courage and respect during our joint journey."

I sent this very logical letter to him, and he liked my carefully tailored strategy. Yet, I kept one burning question in my heart: shall I leave my beloved or not? Is healing really possible after so many tears and so much disrespect? I walked leisurely around Cusco in the afternoon, and rest up before my big day in Machu Picchu, the lost city of the Inca civilization. Built in the fifteenth century and later abandoned, Machu Picchu is renowned for its dry-stone walls, intriguing buildings and temples with astronomical alignments, and spiritual mystery with regard to its exact former use.

The next day, I joined a tour, led by a local guide to learn more about Machu Picchu. First I admire the Inti Watana, a notable ritual stone associated with the astronomic clock or calendar of the Incas. Then the Temple of the Sun, the Temple of the Moon, and the Room of the Three Windows pulled our attention. Later, I gazed into the water mirrors and searched my inner heart.

I wore black yoga trousers, a black turtleneck, and a black shawl to keep me warm. I learned that black is the color of purity for the Incas because it does not mix with the other colors. That's an interesting discovery, because in most cultures today, white symbolizes purity. The more I learned about Machu Picchu, the more mysterious it became. Why was it abandoned? Why was it not destroyed by the conquerors? Were sacrifices just for animals or were humans also sacrificed at the peaks of Machu Picchu? Was it a palace housing the ruling classes, or an astronomical observatory, or did it serve a different purpose? Sometimes, it is better to enjoy the mystery.

On the way back, I decided to climb up for a second time. I simply liked to sit quietly and gaze at the Lost City. As I climbed, I chatted with three young tourists. They were from Mexico and were interested in Istanbul, the city of two continents. I gave one of them my card so he could contact me when he decided to visit Turkey. I asked him where he is from and his response amazed me.

"Guelatao, a small village in Oaxaca."

I knew exactly where Guelatao is. I stayed there during a New Year's holiday more than eighteen years ago. My beloved had worked with the indigenous communities there on land rights. It was there that I had discovered his nickname, Mariposa, which means butterfly.

That's a strange coincidence, I thought. I couldn't wait to tell him. I started climbing slowly. There were considerably fewer people on the tracks, and the light was gentle in the afternoon. I climbed up and found a corner in the shade to take off my shoes. I settled into an observant, listening mode. I gazed over the intriguing shapes of Machu Picchu from the top. I got a feeling of harmony and a desire to go beyond the obvious categorizations of life.

There were only a handful of visitors left at the top of Machu Picchu when the guards start asking us to leave. One of them instructed me to put my shoes on. Apparently, it is forbidden to be barefoot in Machu Picchu, which I did not know before. I always take my shoes off in a new place and take my iconic "the world under my feet" photos. I walked slowly down, and then noticed the queue for the return buses. It went on and on. At least two hundred people were waiting, and the rain was getting heavier, and the road was turning into sticky mud.

I walked toward the end of the queue, but I saw a familiar face. I knew her, but I could not think of her name or where we met. I took a quick few steps, as I had to find out. I ran toward her, because she is at the beginning of the queue, so she might board the second bus. I stood in front of her and say, "I know you. Do you remember me?"

She said, "Billur, is that you? What are you doing here?"
Then I stare at the man standing behind her. I know him, too. He is her husband.

"I am Raylynn," she says.

Of course I remember her. She, my beloved, and I all worked together exactly twenty years ago for the United Nations in Central Asia. We had not seen each other for at least eighteen years. We did not know each other's whereabouts either. My mind races back to the sweet moments of my first encounter with my beloved: the thrill of the first moments of a love story, the first picnic, the first holiday in the mountains, even our first fight, and our first peacemaking in the piano room.

I still couldn't believe that I met her here, after all those years, among thousands of visitors. According to our guide, each day up to five thousand visitors arrive in Machu Picchu. And she was there, right in front of me. What a coincidence!

In a matter of two hours, I had two encounters that brought up fun, loving, special memories with my beloved. Was this the magic of Machu Picchu that people speak of? I boarded the train for the return journey. It was getting dark, and I was seated next to a kind-looking woman who was traveling with her husband and their teenage son. I look at the son's face; his smile is bright, like the sunshine drawn in a child's drawings. He is wearing a long aboriginal earring, and his curly hair and bright smile make him look almost like a cherub. As we talked, we found many common interests, and three hours passed with jokes, amazement, and great companionship. "I should visit them in Brazil," I thought. I asked their names, and I could not believe my ears. That sunshine boy had the same name as my beloved.

It is almost unbelievable, but I received three clear signs from the spirits of Machu Picchu. The question I had posed the night before during my casual meditation about leaving him had been answered.

After the seventeen-hour journey to Machu Picchu, I walked into my hotel room exhausted, but not yet ready to sleep. I was supposed to list all the grievances, hurtful behaviors, and emotional bruises left in me. But for some reason, I could not. I did not. I felt absolutely no desire to go back to the past. It's the past...passed.

It seems that the logical, step-by-step healing path was no longer necessary for me anymore. I wondered why. I did not necessarily understand that magical shift in me, but I accepted it. Was it because the butterflies landed in my hands in Machu Picchu? Did those wonderful creatures switch my mode of being to my spirit: out is the mind and in is the heart?

Instead of starting with the first step of the healing process I'd designed meticulously with my mind, I started from the last step: appreciation and a thank-you note. Heart-full living in action. The response I got is a balm on my wounds.

"Dearest soul mate and partner in life,

A heartful thank you for your thank-you letter that touched me deeply.

Thank you for your resilient love toward me in the good times and (very) bad times, for keeping the gate of compassion and understanding open.

Thank you for having gifted our family with this most amazing child.

Thank you for taking utmost care of our daughter and nurturing her with love, understanding, advice, new ideas, curiosity, and beauty.

Thank you for your determination and courage to free yourself from the chains of grievances and look courageously toward the future.

Thank you for giving me another chance to rebound in my heart, spirit, and mind, and stand in front of you as a man of values, vision, heart.

Thank you for your enthusiasm to embrace family, life, people, your aspirations with so much passion and interest.

Because I have much admiration and gratitude for who YOU are and what you do for me and for our daughter.

I love you and cherish you in my heart, mind, and spirit, and I cannot express it enough.

We have been able to face all kinds of difficulties and hurdles, and we can overcome this crisis together.

And therefore I commit:

To make all efforts to become again a whole round partner, intellectual, sexual, material, spiritual, parent.

To express regularly and wholeheartedly my love and appreciation toward you.

To dedicate time and efforts to strengthen our unique bond.

To end all sexual encounters that create separation between us.

Let our letters merge their energies and dedication and commitment under the auspicious blessings of Cusco and Machu Picchu.

I wish you a marvelous journey in the land of Lincoln and Freedom with new, inspiring people.

I kiss you, je t'embrasse, te abrazo with love and tenderness."

I briefly responded at the airport. Once I felt he was open, receptive, and empathetic to my pain, and he was able and willing to face and soothe it, I had no reason to hold on to those painful memories. They were acknowledged, and I felt free. All of a sudden my obsession, or preoccupation, of the last ten months and all the hurtful deeds were not important or relevant anymore.

What I had been seeking, in the last ten months, had been given to me in one shot: a deep sense of liberation, harmony, and inner freedom. The past had blown away with the Machu Picchu wind and I was free to walk into my future.